ALGORITHMIC TRADING IN CRYPTO

ENGINEERINGROBO

LIMIT OF LIABILITY/ DISCLAIMER OF WARRANTY

Copyright © 2023 by EngineeringRobo

All rights reserved.

While the author has used his best efforts in preparing this book, he makes no representations or warranties with respect to the accuracy or completeness of the contents of this book and specifically disclaims any implied warranties of merchantability or fitness for a particular purpose.

Trading and investing involve substantial risk. Financial loss, even above the amount invested, is possible and common. Seek the services of a competent professional before investing or trading with money.

By reading this book, you agree that use of the information in this book is entirely at your own risk. The author is not a registered investment advisor. You understand and acknowledge that there is a very high degree of risk involved in trading cryptocurrencies, futures, and securities. Past results of any individual trader are not indicative of future returns by that trader and are not indicative of future returns which may be realized by you.

The content in Algorithmic Trading in Crypto with EngineeringRobo is intended to be used for informational and educational purposes only and should not be construed as investment advice. The author may hold positions in the cryptos, futures, or industries discussed here. You should not rely solely on this information in making any investment. The information in this course should only be used as a starting point for doing additional independent research in order to allow you to form your own opinion regarding investments and trading strategies.

Do not assume that the information in this manual will result in you being a profitable trader or that it will prevent losses. Past results are not necessarily indicative of future results. You should never trade with money you cannot afford to lose.

Factual statements in this book are made as of the date the book was created and are subject to change without notice.

Hypothetical or Simulated Performance Results have Certain Inherent Limitations. Unlike an Actual Performance Record, Simulated Results do not Represent Actual Trading. Also, Since The Trades have not Actually been Executed, The Results may have under- or over-compensated for the Impact, If any, of Certain Market Factors, Such as Lack of Liquidity. Simulated Trading Programs in General are also Subject to the Fact that they are designed with the benefit of Hindsight. No representation is being made that any Account will or is likely to achieve profits or losses similar to those shown.

Paperback ISBN 978-1-7388071-1-6

eBook ISBN 978-1-7388071-0-9

To my lovely Grandmother, Durdu Coskun
(March 10, 1923 – December 21, 2022)

The most selfless woman I've ever met, you are
deeply missed, rest in peace.

"There is a time to go long, a time to go short and a time to go fishing."

- Jesse Livermore

"In this business, if you're good, you're right six times out of ten. You're never going to be right nine times out of ten."

- Peter Lynch

"Do not anticipate and move without market confirmation - being a little late in your trade is your insurance that you are right or wrong."

- Jesse Livermore

"Past performance is the best predictor of success."

- Jim Simons

"I always laugh at people who say, 'I've never met a rich technician.' I love that! It's such an arrogant, nonsensical response. I used fundamentals for nine years and got rich as a technician."

- Martin Schwartz

TABLE OF CONTENTS

ABOUT THE AUTHOR — 1

INTRODUCTION — 4

PART I — 7

- WHAT IS CRYPTOCURRENCY? — 8
- IS TRADING CRYPTO PROFITABLE? — 9
- BRIEF HISTORY OF BITCOIN — 11
- WHAT IS A CRYPTO WALLET? — 12
- HOW DO CRYPTO WALLETS WORK? — 13
- TYPES OF CRYPTO WALLETS? — 14
- HOW TO SECURE YOUR CRYPTO ACCOUNT? — 15
- WHAT IS THE BEST DAY TO BUY CRYPTOCURRENCY? — 17
- CRYPTOCURRENCY CATEGORIES — 19
- BEST CRYPTOCURRENCIES TO INVEST IN ACCORDING TO HEDGE FUNDS IN 2022 — 21
- CRYPTO FUNDRASING MODELS — 25

PART II — 27

- ARE YOU ASPIRING TO BE A TRADER? — 28
- WHAT IS A TRADING STRATEGY? — 28
- WHAT TYPE OF CRYPTO TRADER ARE YOU? — 30
- WHICH IS BETTER FOR ME? — 35
- DAY TRADING vs SCALPING vs SWING TRADING — 37
- THE UPS AND DOWNS OF TRADING CRYPTOCURRENCIES — 39
- AVERAGING DOWN: A TRADING STRATEGY TO AVOID OR EMBRACE? — 42
- HOW TO CALCULATE POSITION SIZE IN TRADING? — 44
- WHAT ARE THE FUTURES TRADING RULES YOU LIVE BY? — 46
- WHAT ADVICE WOULD YOU GIVE TO NOVICE TRADERS? — 48

PART III — 51

- HOW TO GET THE MAXIMUM RETURNS FROM CRYPTO MARKET CYCLES? — 52
- WHAT IS THE BEST TIMEFRAME TO TRADE CRYPTO? — 54
- LEVERAGE IN CRYPTO MARKET: A DOUBLE-EDGED SWORD — 56
- HIGH LEVERAGE RISKS AND BENEFITS — 58
- HOW TO TRADE LIKE A HEDGE FUND TRADER IN CRYPTO? — 60

PART IV — 63

- WHAT IS TECHNICAL ANALYSIS? — 64
- 4 EASY STEPS TO BE A MASTER AT TECHNICAL ANALYSIS — 65
- CHART PATTERNS CHEAT SHEET — 67
- BUY AT THE SUPPORT AND SELL AT THE RESISTANCE — 69
- FIBONACCI LEVELS — 70
- MOVING AVERAGE TRADING SECRETS — 70
- SO WHY DO PEOPLE USE MOVING AVERAGES? — 71

PART V — 73

- IS ALGOTRADING THE FUTURE OF CRYPTO TRADING? — 74
- WHAT IS ENGINEERINGROBO? — 76
- WHY DO YOU NEED ENGINEERINGROBO? — 77
- ENGINEERINGROBO'S FORMULA — 79
- ROBO ADVISORS BACKTESTING — 81
- DON'T USE MORE THAN 3 ROBO SIGNALS AT THE SAME TIME. WHY? — 85
- HOW TO PICK WINNING CRYPTOCURRENCIES — 87
- HOW TO USE ENGINEERINGROBO ON CHARTS — 89
- BULL MARKET CASE STUDIES — 92
- BEAR MARKET CASE STUDIES — 93
- ENGINEERINGROBO'S CRYPTO PORTFOLIO MANAGEMENT TOOL — 94
- DEVELOP YOUR OWN STRATEGY IN ENGINEERINGROBO — 96

PART VI — 99

- BITCOIN RALLIES MOST LIKELY START IN OCTOBER. SO, WHAT IS NEXT? — 100

FOCUS ON WHAT YOU CAN CONTROL AS A TRADER	102
THE ART OF EXIT LEVELS - CRYPTO PUMP & DUMP	108
IS FUNDAMENTAL NEWS FUNDAMENTALLY USELESS IN BULL MARKETS?	111
IS FUNDAMENTAL NEWS FUNDAMENTALLY USELESS IN BEAR MARKETS?	113
CRYPTOCURRENCY TAX GUIDE	115
TOP FINANCE MOVIES EVERY TRADER SHOULD WATCH	116
BEST TRADING AND INVESTING BOOKS TO READ	118

PART VII   121

HOW TO INVEST $1 MILLION IN TODAY'S MARKET	122
HOW I HAVE LOST AROUND $88,000 IN FUTURES MARKET SINCE 2016?	125
HOW ISAAC NEWTON LOST $4 MILLION IN THE SOUTH SEA BUBBLE OF 1720?	127
STRESS MANAGEMENT IN THE TRADING DAY	129
CRYPTO MARKET CYCLES	132

PART VIII   135

THE SUMMARY OF BITCOIN MOVEMENT BETWEEN 2011 AND 2013	136
THE SUMMARY OF BITCOIN MOVEMENT BETWEEN 2013 AND 2016	138
THE SUMMARY OF BITCOIN MOVEMENT BETWEEN 2016 AND 2020	140
THE SUMMARY OF BITCOIN MOVEMENT BETWEEN 2020 AND 2023	142

PART IX   145

FREQUENTLY ASKED QUESTIONS	146
10 IMPORTANT WEBSITES TO CHECK REGULARLY	151
MYTHS AND MISCONCEPTIONS FOR CRYPTO INVESTORS	153

AFTERWORD	**156**
INDEX	**158**
REFERENCES	**159**
TO GET FUTURE UPDATES, FOLLOW US ON…	**160**

ABOUT THE AUTHOR

I am a graduate of Electrical and Electronics Engineering with a Bachelor of Science (B.Sc.). During my years at university, I always believed that finance was not just all about money and the stock market. It was about connecting people and improving the world. Since then, I have had a high level of interest in financial technology.

I am a graduate of Electrical and Electronics Engineering with a Bachelor of Science (B.Sc.). During my years at university, I always believed that finance was not just all about money and the stock market. It was about connecting people and improving the world. Since then, I have had a high level of interest in financial technology.

I bought my first Bitcoin in November 2013 for $200, following my friend's advice. At that time, $200 was worth over 20 hours of my work. So, it was big money for me. That is why I could not invest more. I also sold my one Bitcoin a few months later when Bitcoin doubled its price.

Yes, I am an Engineer but

☞ I was not a tech-savvy guy

☞ I was not an investor

☞ I did not have any financial vision

☞ I did not have any financial literacy at that time

That is why I read many books, articles and listened to podcasts about finance between 2013 and 2016. At the beginning of 2016, I knew what to do but I did not know where to start. In November 2016, I decided to learn about the crypto market. At the beginning, I made so many mistakes, for example, bought at the top and sold at the bottom.

I lost money while all the coins were gaining from 2x to 10x. I understood the importance of technical analysis (TA). I started following traders on social media, but I was just doing copy trading without understanding the trading mindset. I lost so much money again.

In May 2017, I decided to take trading seriously. I studied a lot to understand every single detail about TA. However, I did not make life-changing money. I even lost money!

Why? Because I did not know the importance of

→ Market Cycles

→ Crypto Portfolio Management

→ Money Management

→ Risk Management

→ Lifespan of The Cryptocurrencies

→ Algorithmic Trading

2018 was brutal. It destroyed me! It destroyed my dream perspective of cryptocurrencies. I "married" many altcoins (alternative coins to Bitcoin) by listening to other people. I hoped they would recover, but 94% of them never did. No one told me that the coins can possibly drop to zero. Everyone was saying " The coins will recover again ". It never happened...

When it comes to 2019, I felt something different. The crypto market was moving differently. Most of them were pumping-and-dumping at the same time. It was so unusual for me and many traders. It took me six months to understand what was going on!

Algorithmic Trading & High-Frequency Trading (HFT) became part of the crypto market. I understood that in crypto, we were not trading against people anymore. We were trading against Robots! Robots were making 50% (now over 70%) of the trades and bringing 70% (now 90%) of the volume to the crypto market. My trading strategy totally changed when I learned this.

As Charles Darwin noted, "It is not the strongest of the species that survives, nor the most intelligent; it is the one most adaptable to change." That is why I spent over seven months, from May 2019 until January 2020, with a team of four software developers creating EngineeringRobo. Why? To adapt to the New Market Conditions.

Since then, over 550 people have been using EngineeringRobo daily to increase their trading success all over the world.

INTRODUCTION

Between January 2019 and March 2022, making money in the crypto market was incredibly easy. In fact, it was almost impossible to lose money. At the beginning of 2019, Bitcoin's price was about $4,000. When the coronavirus pandemic shut down the economy and stirred up fears of inflationary pressure on the U.S. dollar, bitcoin's price started to accelerate in its upward climb. Between January and December 2020, the cost of 1 Bitcoin increased by almost 300%. By the end of the year, Bitcoin reached $29,374 — the highest it had ever been.

Bitcoin doubled its value in 2021, but in January 2022 it saw a big drop that erased almost all the previous year's gains. We saw Bitcoin skyrocket to an all-time high of over $64,000 in the first half of 2021, then just as quickly fall back below $30,000 over the summer. Bitcoin hit another all-time high of over $69,000 in November, but by January 2022, it dropped back below $34,000. It approached $48,000 in March 2022; how could you possibly lose money?

People signed up with online exchanges and began trading cryptocurrencies with little or no training. Most of them lacked a predefined strategy or even the knowledge that they needed one in order to succeed. These traders would simply search for the latest meme crypto, buy it, watch it rise in price, sell it, and collect their profit. It could not have been any easier.

As we all know, there is no free lunch in life—what goes up must come down. That is exactly what the crypto market did, starting in May 2022. A few of us did survive. In fact, with the decreased competition, we thrived. And as we started sharing our secrets of success, our ranks began to grow. EngineeringRobo reached over 550 members worldwide. Before I explain the EngineeringRobo system and how trading works, I want to make a few things clear.

First and foremost, this is not a get-rich-quick system. I am not promising that you will go from homeless to living in a mansion in six months by trading. That simply is not a realistic expectation. One of the primary tenets of my trading system is to set realistic goals. Another important tenet of this system is humility. Very often, people approach the topic of trading with the mindset, "I'm smarter than most people, so I'll make so much money overnight." Well, if that is how you are thinking, get that idea out of your head immediately!

Quite honestly, I have no idea which cryptocurrencies are safe investments, and which are bad ones. And guess what? I do not care. I am not in the business of investing good cryptos. I am in the business of making money in the crypto market, and as you will soon discover, the two are not necessarily the same. So how do I pick my cryptos then? I leave my ego at the door and play "follow my system and EngineeringRobo signals." I learn what the market makers and insiders are doing and mimic their movements. If they're buying XYZ coin and expect a $2 bounce, then I buy XYZ coin with them and sell when they do by confirming with the EngineeringRobo signals. In this book, I'll also show you how to find this information and, more importantly, how to act on it.

The last and arguably most crucial piece of the puzzle is discipline. Like anything else in life, the discipline also requires some work and effort. Sadly, this is something that some people do not understand, and they quickly jump to the conclusion that the system does not work.

EngineeringRobo works. But it will only work for you if you put in the time, effort, and discipline required. To work at it, you must be regimented. Without these critical tools, you will not be able to make money—at least not consistently. I am not trying to scare you away from crypto trading. I just want you, the reader, to understand that success will only come to those who make the commitment.

Of course, there are no guarantees in this book or in life for that matter. I am confident that after reading Algorithmic Trading in Crypto with EngineeringRobo, you will begin to understand the fundamentals which every trader should know. However, without further practice in all the subject matter contained in the book, you will not become a consistent and profitable trader.

Happy Trading!

PART I

WHAT IS CRYPTOCURRENCY?	8
IS TRADING CRYPTO PROFITABLE?	9
BRIEF HISTORY OF BITCOIN	11
WHAT IS A CRYPTO WALLET?	12
HOW DO CRYPTO WALLETS WORK?	13
TYPES OF CRYPTO WALLETS?	14
HOW TO SECURE YOUR CRYPTO ACCOUNT?	15
WHAT IS THE BEST DAY TO BUY CRYPTOCURRENCY?	17
CRYPTOCURRENCY CATEGORIES	19
BEST CRYPTOCURRENCIES TO INVEST IN ACCORDING TO HEDGE FUNDS IN 2022	21
CRYPTO FUNDRASING MODELS	25

If you want to learn how to trade cryptocurrency with algorithmic trading, you are in the right place. There are mountains of information available on the internet, which could easily overwhelm anyone, including a seasoned trader. To help you out, we have created this detailed guide to cryptocurrency trading for our EngineeringRobo members.

WHAT IS CRYPTOCURRENCY?

Simply put, cryptocurrencies (also known as digital currencies, cryptos, virtual assets, or digital assets) are digital forms of currencies. They can be used to pay for goods and services just like conventional currencies. Like how the traditional forms of currencies can be traded against each other on the forex, cryptocurrencies can also be traded against specific pairs on specialized platforms called cryptocurrency exchanges.

The difference is that, unlike conventional currencies such as the U.S. dollar, cryptocurrencies are often not controlled by a single entity.

They are also secured using complex cryptography coupled with a new form of online public ledger called a blockchain. It is distributed to anyone and everyone interested in having a copy. More than 21,960 cryptocurrencies currently exist at the time of writing.

IS TRADING CRYPTO PROFITABLE?

Crypto trading is profitable but only if done correctly. Follow the steps, strategies, and tips shared throughout our guide, and you will be in a better position to make profitable trades. And a golden rule:

Plan your trade, trade your plan.

Never Forget: 90/90/90 trading rule.

90% of traders will lose 90% of their account value within 90 days.

1. No matter how much profit you make; what matters is how much you **keep.**
2. No matter how much you keep, what matters is how much you **re-invest.**
3. No matter how much you re-invested, what matters is your total **return on investment (ROI).**

#	Jan	Feb	Mar	Apr	May	Jun	Jul	Aug	Sep	Oct	Nov	Dec	Average	Total
2022	-16.7%	12.18%	5.41%	-17.3%	-15.56%	-37.32%	16.95%	-13.99%	-3.1%	6.41%	-16.26%	N/A	-6.75%	-81.02%
2021	14.37%	36.41%	30.11%	-1.78%	-35.38%	-6.09%	18.63%	13.42%	-7.02%	39.9%	-7.22%	-18.75%	6.38%	76.6%
2020	29.91%	-8.62%	-24.94%	34.56%	9.57%	-3.38%	24.06%	2.74%	-7.46%	28.04%	42.77%	46.97%	14.52%	174.22%
2019	-7.34%	11.04%	7.49%	29.7%	60.85%	26.41%	-6.81%	-4.84%	-13.65%	10.48%	-17.55%	-4.64%	7.60%	91.14%
2018	-25.88%	0.67%	-32.86%	33.25%	-18.85%	-14.71%	20.79%	-9%	-5.67%	-4.06%	-36.54%	-8.18%	-8.42%	-101.04%
2017	0.22%	23.18%	-9.26%	25.28%	70.38%	7.7%	16.23%	64.23%	-7.91%	47.94%	54.18%	39.25%	27.62%	331.42%
2016	-13.98%	17.95%	-4.71%	7.91%	17.92%	26.68%	-7.19%	-7.72%	5.97%	14.89%	6.27%	29.75%	7.81%	93.74%
2015	-31.34%	16.27%	-3.9%	-3.43%	-2.31%	14.92%	17.42%	-19.43%	2.68%	31.92%	21.44%	13.75%	4.02%	48.22%
2014	16.49%	-38.87%	-22.53%	0.22%	40.9%	1.15%	-7.18%	-18.28%	-19.43%	-12.96%	10.97%	-15.12%	-5.39%	-64.64%
2013	51.07%	63.55%	178.7%	49.66%	-7.48%	-24.31%	8.92%	32.76%	0.64%	48.82%	470.94%	-33.15%	70.01%	840.12%
2012	16.1%	-11.31%	0%	0%	4.65%	29.15%	39.76%	8.66%	22.05%	-9.68%	12.23%	7.48%	9.92%	119.09%
2011	73.33%	65.38%	-8.77%	346.09%	149.71%	84.21%	-17.08%	-38.58%	-37.32%	-36.77%	-8.62%	58.92%	52.54%	630.5%
2010	0%	0%	0%	0%	0%	0%	0%	0%	0%	210.99%	0%	44.09%	21.26%	255.08%
2009	0%	0%	0%	0%	0%	0%	0%	0%	0%	0%	0%	0%	0.0%	0%
Average	7.59%	13.42%	8.20%	36.01%	19.59%	7.46%	8.18%	0.73%	-5.01%	26.79%	38.04%	11.39%	12.31%	172.39%
Total	106.25%	187.83%	114.74%	504.16%	274.19%	104.4%	114.5%	10.28%	-70.08%	375.04%	532.61%	159.51%	172.39%	2413.43%

The monthly return of Bitcoin since 2010

BRIEF HISTORY OF BITCOIN

It all began in the 1990s when American cryptographer, David Chaum, created what was considered the first kind of online money in the Netherlands: DigiCash. He created DigiCash as an extension of an encryption algorithm that was considered popular during those times, which was RSA. The technology was able to generate a huge amount of attention from the media all over the world.

It became so popular that Microsoft tried to buy DigiCash for $180 million with the intention of placing DigiCash on every computer in the world that ran on the Windows operating system. One of the crucial mistakes Chaum and his company made was to reject Microsoft's $180 million offer. After several years of trials, DigiCash wasn't catching on with the general public. The banks that got on board were experimenting but did not really push the technology. All of those crucial mistakes eventually led to the demise of DigiCash in 1998, when the company went bankrupt.

In the midst of the global financial crisis of 2008, somebody under the name of Satoshi Nakamoto designed Bitcoin. He released the first Bitcoin software that launched the network and the first units of the Bitcoin cryptocurrency. Bitcoin became a new type of digital currency, which was very different from all the others. Bitcoin and DigiCash have little in common. Even if every person only used DigiCash for their transactions, banks would still be necessary to offer account balances and confirm transactions. The main difference lies in the fact that Bitcoin is decentralized. Therefore, each participant cannot influence its fate.

There are a lot of people on the network who do not know each other, so it's logical that they do not trust each other. So how can they be sure that payments are carried out and their money will not be stolen?

However, everything was thought out in advance by Satoshi Nakamoto. Suffice to say that Nakamoto's vision for a decentralized currency held true, solving many problems. By the way, the identity of Satoshi Nakamoto is still shrouded in mystery. Several attempts have been made to disclose it because some people believe that Satoshi Nakamoto is a group of people rather than one person. However, none of these attempts has proved successful.

🎯 **Pro – Tip**: Do you want to invest in Bitcoin? Historically, the best months to buy Bitcoin are from October to mid-December. Good to fair months are from mid-January to May. The summer months have less trading volume because traders are inactive (on vacation). However, it is possible to find good trades every day by following EngineeringRobo signals.

WHAT IS A CRYPTO WALLET?

Cryptocurrency wallets, or simply crypto wallets, are places where traders store secure digital codes needed to interact with a blockchain. They do not actively store your cryptocurrencies despite what their name may lead you to believe.

Crypto wallets need to locate the crypto associated with your address in the blockchain, which is why they must interact with it. In fact, crypto wallets are not as much a wallet as they are ledgers: They function as an owner's identity and account on a blockchain network and provide access to transaction history.

HOW DO CRYPTO WALLETS WORK?

When someone sends Bitcoin, Ethereum, Dogecoin, or any other type of digital currency to your crypto wallet, you are not actually transferring any coins. What they are doing is signing off ownership thereof to your wallet's address. That is to say, they are confirming that the crypto on the blockchain no longer belongs to their address but yours. Two digital codes are necessary for this process: a public key and a private key.

A public key is a string of letters and numbers automatically generated by the crypto wallet provider. For example, a public key could look like this: B1Robo539i7L822can5oY5xgV614.

A private key is another string of numbers and letters but one that only the owner of the wallet should know.

Think of a crypto wallet as an email account. To receive an email, you need to give people your email address. This would be your public key in the case of crypto wallets, and you need to share it with others to be part of any blockchain transaction. However, you would never give someone the password to access your email account. For crypto wallets, that password is equivalent to your private key, which under no circumstances should be shared with another person.

Using these two keys, crypto wallet users can participate in transactions without compromising the integrity of the currency being traded or of the transaction itself. The public key assigned to your digital wallet must match your private key to authenticate any funds sent or received. Once both keys are verified, the balance in your crypto wallet will increase or decrease accordingly.

TYPES OF CRYPTO WALLETS?

Mobile wallets: For those actively using Bitcoin to pay for goods in shops or make trades face-to-face daily, a mobile crypto wallet is an essential tool. It runs as an app on your smartphone, storing private keys and allowing you to pay, trade, and store crypto with the phone.

Desktop wallets: Desktop wallets are downloaded and installed onto your computer, storing the private keys on your hard drive or solid-state drives (SSD). By definition, they are more secure than online and mobile wallets, as they don't rely on third parties for their data and are harder to steal.

Web wallets (exchange wallets): Web wallets (a form of Bitcoin hot wallet) store your private keys on a server, which is constantly online and controlled by a third party. Different services offer different features, some of which can link to mobile and desktop wallets and replicate your addresses across the devices you own. Much like mobile wallets, e-wallets enable their users to access their funds on the go from any device connected to the internet. The organizations running the website can gain access to your private keys, thus gaining total control of your funds.

Most e-wallets operate on exchanges, and there have been instances of exchanges shutting down and making off with their users' funds like FTX, QuadrigaCX, Thodex, CoinBene, etc. Exchange wallets are also frequently targeted by hackers because they are accessible using only your email address and password.

Hardware wallets: A crypto hardware wallet is a rather unique type of crypto wallet that stores private keys in a secure physical device. It is believed to be the most secure way of storing any number of cryptocurrencies. Unlike paper-based wallets, which must be imported to software at some point, hardware wallets can be used securely and interactively. They are immune to computer viruses, as the funds stored cannot be transferred out of the device in plaintext and, in most instances, their software is open source.

Most hardware wallets have screens that add another layer of security, as they can be used to verify and display important wallet details. For instance, a screen can generate a recovery phrase and confirm the amount and address of the payment you wish to make. So, as long as you invest in an authentic device made by a trustworthy and competent manufacturer, your funds will be safe and secure.

Pro-tip: Never purchase a crypto hardware wallet from any used item marketplaces.

HOW TO SECURE YOUR CRYPTO ACCOUNT?

Cryptocurrency can be rewarding but dangerous, especially with so many cybersecurity risks. So how should you protect your crypto?

When it comes to keeping your cryptocurrencies secure, the blockchain industry today provides many security measures. From trading to storing and using your crypto, simple tips are effective in keeping your funds safe.

If you signed up for your exchange or chosen trading method, follow standard good practices to keep your account safe. These tips are no different from those you would use for your online bank account or other sensitive information. Preventing people from getting access to your account and its funds is easy by:

1. Using a strong password you regularly change. The password should not include identifiable personal information like your date of birth, for example. Make sure it is also long, is unique to that account, and contains symbols, numbers, and lowercase and uppercase letters.

2. Enabling Two-Factor Authentication (2FA). If your password is compromised, 2FA using your mobile device, authenticator app, or YubiKey acts as a second level of protection. You need to use both your password and the 2FA method together when logging in.

3. Watching out for phishing attacks and scams via email, social media, and private messages. Fraudsters frequently impersonate exchanges and trusted individuals to try and steal your funds.

4. For maximum safety, consider investing in a Virtual Private Network (VPN). A good VPN will encrypt your communications and hide your online activities from potential intruders while hiding all cryptographic activities from your Internet Service Provider (ISP).

Number of Characters	Numbers Only	Lowercase Letters	Upper and Lowercase Letters	Numbers, Upper and Lowercase Letters	Numbers, Upper and Lowercase Letters, Symbols
4	Instantly	Instantly	Instantly	Instantly	Instantly
5	Instantly	Instantly	Instantly	Instantly	Instantly
6	Instantly	Instantly	Instantly	Instantly	Instantly
7	Instantly	Instantly	2 secs	7 secs	31 secs
8	Instantly	Instantly	2 mins	7 mins	39 mins
9	Instantly	10 secs	1 hour	7 hours	2 days
10	Instantly	4 mins	3 days	3 weeks	5 months
11	Instantly	2 hours	5 months	3 years	34 years

The chart shows how long it takes to crack your password.

How Secure is Your Password? Check out here, https://www.passwordmonster.com

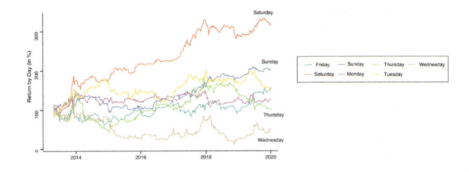

WHAT IS THE BEST DAY TO BUY CRYPTOCURRENCY?

Based on my crypto trading experience since 2016, there is no better day to buy cryptocurrencies. You may never be able to predict 100% the best time to buy Bitcoin. However, if you know what to look for on the market and elsewhere, you can make an educated guess.

If I really have to choose a day, the best day of the week to buy cryptocurrency is Saturday when prices are the lowest. Sunday is the next best day of the week overall. The reduced trading volume on weekends is the primary reason for getting discounted Bitcoin prices.

After that, prices rise with Monday being the most expensive day to buy cryptocurrency. In the best-case scenario, you should sell Bitcoin on weekdays.

☞ When demand is high, prices will be high, too.

☞ Business hours tend to be the worst times to buy Bitcoin because more people are trading.

☞ Media coverage of cryptocurrency can also have a massive impact on the value of Bitcoin. It could be possible to experience a big drop on Monday if we get negative news over the weekend.

You can also compare the days here:
https://www.whatifihodl.com/crypto-profit-today-calculator.html

It is important to remember that even though the history of cryptocurrency is displayed, it should not be used solely to make predictions. That's why we need technical charts and EngineeringRobo to improve our trading strategy.

You should think of EngineeringRobo as your car headlights on the road. When you drive your car in the dark without headlights, you have a high chance of getting into a car accident. If your lights are on, there is still some risk, but you are lowering the chance of getting into a car accident.

Nearly 60% of US consumers expect to use a robo-advisor by 2025, according to research from Charles Schwab. Additionally, 60% of current robo-advisor users are millennials who are expected to have $20 trillion of assets globally by 2030, per CB Insights. As that wealth grows, more money will likely flow into robo-advisors, especially as they often offer such services at a cheaper price than incumbent wealth managers.

One of the biggest advantages of a robo-advisor is the removal of human emotion from financial markets. When trading, people are susceptible to emotions that lead to irrational decisions. EngineeringRobo does not have to think or feel good to make a trade. If conditions are met, it sends buy signals. When the trade goes the wrong way or hits a profit target, it sends sell signals. It does not get angry at the market or feel invincible after making a few good trades.

CRYPTOCURRENCY CATEGORIES

→ **Currencies:** BTC, LTC, ZCASH, BCH, DOGE, OMG, DGB, XEM, XNO, BCN

→ **Smart Contracts:** ETH, BNB, ADA, SOL, AVAX, EOS, XTZ, ZIL, HBAR

→ **Memes:** DOGE, SHIBA, MONA, SAFEMOON, FLOKI

→ **Privacy:** XMR, ZCASH, DASH, DCR, XVG, PIVX, FIRO, RLC, BEAM, BCN, SCRT, TRTL

→ **Metaverse:** MANA, SAND, AXS, ALICE, TLM, THETA

→ **Web 3:** DOT, LINK, FIL, BAT, ANT, OCEAN, OXT, RAD, TRB, LIT, POND

→ **Internet of Things:** ICP, IOTX, MIOTA, HNT, IOST, NKN

→ **Artificial Intelligence:** OCEAN, FET, NMR, GRT, PHA, DATA, GLM, AION

→ **Storage:** FIL, BTT, HOT, SC, STORJ, AR, REP

→ **Oracle:** LINK, UMA, BAND, TRB, REB

→ **Media:** THETA, AUDIO, STEEM, MOVIEBLOC, RDD

→ **Stable coins:** USDT, USDC, BUSD, DAI, UST, GUSD

→ **Enterprise Solutions:** XRP, XLM, NEO, ANKR, LSK, STRAX

→ **Scaling:** MATIC, BOBA, ONE, ZRX, ARPA, FTM

→ **Defi & Yield Farming:** UNI, CAKE, YFI, 1INCH, SRM, SUSHI, BAKE, BAL, CRV, UMA, XVS, ALPACA, FLM

→ **Decentralized Exchange:** UNI, CAKE, 1INCH, BNT, SRM, DODO

→ **Gaming:** AXS, PLA, GMT, ALICE, BAKE, WINK

→ **Collectibles:** NFTs: APE, AXS, WAXP, APENFT, ROSE, SUPER, SLP, RARE, DEGO, FLOW, FIO

→ **Identity Tokens:** ONT, CVC, KEY, KILT

→ **Asset Management:** MLN, DEXE, HMQ, WINGS, VGX

→ **Lending & Borrowing:** AAVE, MKR, KAVA, COMP, ALPACA

→ **Master nodes:** DASH, ZEN, SYS, STRAX, PIVX, XDN

→ **Logistics:** VET, XYO, AMB, WTC, PPT, SHIP

→ **Fan Token:** CHZ, ALPINE, PSG, BAR, GAL, CITY, ASR, JUV

→ **Cybersecurity:** UTK, CTK, QSP

→ **Exchange Tokens:** BNB, FTT, CRO, KCS, HT, GT, WOO, PLA

🎯 **Pro-tip:** Another way to diversify your crypto portfolio is to invest in cryptocurrency projects which are focused on different industries.

BEST CRYPTOCURRENCIES TO INVEST IN ACCORDING TO HEDGE FUNDS IN 2022

Cryptocurrency hedge funds are investment funds that pool capital from investors into a group of assets focusing on cryptocurrencies or other decentralized digital assets. Funds are actively managed by experts or insider investors, who charge a fee for the analysis and selection of investment opportunities.

→ **Binance Labs Capital**

BTC, ETH, BNB, MATIC, SAND, KAVA, BTT, ONE, 1INCH, AUDIO, APT, ROSE, BAND, REEF, CHZ, FTX, LUNA, etc.

→ **Coinbase Ventures**

BTC, ETH, MATIC, NEAR, UNI, FLOW, CELO, COMP, AUDIO, UMA, DODO, EDG, SNX, RARI, ZRX, FTX, ALGO, LUNA, etc.

→ **Alameda Research**

BTC, ETH, BNB, SOL, FTT, MATIC, UNI, AAVE, COMP, 1INCH, SRM, SUSHI, BAL, DODO, C98, REEF, LEO, OKB, HT, etc.

→ **Huobi Capital**

BTC, ETH, HUOBI, THETA, STX, IOST, ROSE, REN, ELF, ONT, SAND, AMPL, CTXC, CKB, LUNA, etc.

→ **OKEx Blockdream Ventures**

BTC, ETH, SOL, WAXP, OKB, CSPR, XPR, ASTR, METIS, ALGO, etc.

→ **Winklevoss Capital**

BTC, ETH, FIL, XTZ, ZCASH, ROSE, etc.

→ Blockchain.com Ventures

BTC, ETH, DOT, FIL, 1INCH, ZRX, AAVE, NEAR, OGN, THETA, ENJ, ZRX, OXT, LUNA, etc.

→ Andreessen Horowitz Ventures

BTC, ETH, COIN, AVAX, COMP, ICP, CELO, MKR, SAND, UNI, APT, NEAR, HNT, DYDX, SOL, FLOW, etc.

→ Galaxy Digital

BTC, ETH, ADA, SOL, AVAX, DOT, MATIC, ATOM, LTC, LINK, ALGO, XMR, 1INCH, SKL, RAD, DODO, ANC, LUNA, etc.

→ Draper VC

BTC, ETH, XTZ, BNT, MAKER, FCT, etc.

→ Grayscale Investments

BTC, ETH, BAT, BCH, LINK, MANA, ETC, FIL, LTC, ZEN, SOL, XLM, ZEC, etc.

→ Kenetic Capital

BTC, ETH, SOL, DOT, FTT, ALGO, MANA, ZIL, QTUM, ZRX, SRM, WAXP, OXT, GNO, NEAR, HT, KSM, REEF, LUNA, etc.

→ Fabric Ventures

BTC, ETH, DOT, NEAR, MANA, 1INCH, ZRX, OCEAN, OXT, SNT, STX, RAD, KEEP, DATA, RDN, BLT, etc.

→ Animoca Brands Foundation

FLOW, APE, SAND, AXS, SUPER, TLM, MATIC, REQ, etc.

→ **Arrington Capital**

BTC, ETH, XRP, DOT, NEAR, ALGO, ENJ, AR, KAVA, ROSE, ARPA, NEXO, STX, RSR, CELR, MFT, PRO, AMPL, LUNA, etc.

→ **Pantera Capital**

BTC, ETH, ANKR, ZRX, FTT, 1INCH, BAL, XRP, CVC, BAT, FIL, OGN, WAXP, ZCASH, OMG, KYBER, DODO, LUNA, etc.

→ **BoostVC Venture Capital**

BTC, ETH, DOT, XMR, FIL, XTZ, MANA, ZRX, ANT, DNT, ZCASH, KEEP, POP, SKL, RCN, WIT, etc.

→ **DragonFly Capital**

BTC, ETH, AVAX, ATOM, MKR, COMP, 1INCH, ROSE, CELO, COMP, SC, UMA, CKB, NAS, etc.

→ **1confirmation Ventures**

BTC, ETH, DOT, ATOM, MKR, POLY, BAT, REP, DYDX, IRIS, KSM, CKB, NXM, OSMO, RARE, WNXM, etc.

→ **Polychain Capital**

BTC, ETH, AVAX, DOT, ATOM, FIL, XTZ, MKR, COMP, NU, CELO, ICP, POLY, CELO, YFI, ZIL, ZRX, OXT, KEEP, KIN, etc.

→ **a16z Capital**

BTC, ETH, XRP, FIL, COMP, OXT, CELO, MKR, UNI, FLOW, AR, KEEP, RLY, HNS, etc.

→ Fenbushi Capital

DOT, VET, ZCASH, EOS, SC, 1INCH, BAL, DGD, ENJ, FCT, HBAR, ICP, KEEP, MKR, POND, NU, GRT, etc.

→ Spartan Group Capital

BTC, ETH, DOT, MKR, 1INCH, AKRO, BAND, GRT, ACA, ALCX, ALPHA, DYDX, CHESS, YFI, etc.

→ Hashkey Capital

BTC, ETH, DOT, ATOM, XLM, FIL, ZEC, KAVA, ONE, LUNA, STX, CSPR, IOTX, ONE, SKL, CKB, FCT, RCN, LUNA, etc.

→ CMS Holdings

BTC, ETH, SOL, DOT, AVAX, SRM, KSM, FTT, DODO, INJ, CKB, DODO, PERP, LINA, FIDA, HXRO, etc.

→ DeFiance Capital

BTC, ETH, UNI, AAVE, SUSHI, DODO, AXS, SNX, ALPHA, MLN, SWTH, INDEX, MTA, etc.

→ Ex Network Capital

BTC, ETH, DOT, FTT, ATOM, ICP, SRM, SUPER, ALICE, DODO, etc.

→ Three Arrows Capital

BTC, ETH, DOT, AVAX, COMP, AAVE, DODO, BAL, UNI, MINA, NEAR, KSM, KNC, SOL, SNX, YFI, BAL, WOO, LUNA, etc.

CRYPTO FUNDRASING MODELS

Crowdfunding methods can vary, such as using a centralized crypto exchange platform to manage the process (IEO), a DEX Initial Offering (IDO) or simply doing it alone – initial coin offering (ICO).

The history of ICOs dates back to 2013, when Mastercoin launched the first ICO. The platform managed to raise around $600,000 from the process. Ethereum, the second-largest blockchain network by market cap, also launched an ICO in 2014. The ICO raised $18 million within 42 days. ICOs then became an instant hit in the cryptocurrency space, with investors jumping at the opportunity and raising an estimated $4.9 billion by the end of 2017.

In 2017, ICOs were the newest trend for both start-ups and investors, though authorities haven't stopped warning that contributing funds to ICOs is very risky. Still, the idea of winning a fortune, investing less, and profiting more is so appealing that it just can't stop investors. And it shouldn't! In order to avoid scams and fraudulent or manipulative projects — and recognize low-quality campaigns in advance — there are a number of features to evaluate.

IEO full name is Initial Exchange Offering, this is a fundraising event managed by an exchange. Contrary to ICO, IEO fundraising will be conducted on a well-known exchange fundraising platform, such as Binance Launchpad.

A DEX Initial Offering, or IDO for short, is a novel crowdfunding technique that allows cryptocurrency projects to launch their token or native currency through decentralized exchanges (DEXs). DEXs entered the scene in 2019. However, unlike an ICO, where the tokens are sold before being listed on the exchange, in an IDO the tokens are immediately listed on the DEX through which they are released.

However, no one sees a 10-figure IDO matching EOS's $4 billion ICO or Telegram's $1.7 billion raise anytime soon.

Here is a cheat sheet for investors which will help determine the strong sides of an ICO and others so you can decide whether it is worth investing in!

Pro-tip: It must be stressed that though investing in start-ups can be exciting and profitable, there is no need to rush. No matter how you buy crypto, just make sure that you do your research first, and invest wisely!

PART II

ARE YOU ASPIRING TO BE A TRADER?	28
WHAT IS A TRADING STRATEGY?	28
WHAT TYPE OF CRYPTO TRADER ARE YOU?	30
WHICH IS BETTER FOR ME?	35
DAY TRADING vs SCALPING vs SWING TRADING	37
THE UPS AND DOWNS OF TRADING CRYPTOCURRENCIES	39
AVERAGING DOWN: A TRADING STRATEGY TO AVOID OR EMBRACE?	42
HOW TO CALCULATE POSITION SIZE IN TRADING?	44
WHAT ARE THE FUTURES TRADING RULES YOU LIVE BY?	46
WHAT ADVICE WOULD YOU GIVE TO NOVICE TRADERS?	48

ARE YOU ASPIRING TO BE A TRADER?

There are countless ways to profit from trading crypto. Trading strategies help you organize those techniques into a coherent framework that you can follow. This way, you can continually monitor and optimize your cryptocurrency strategy.

The three main schools of thought you will need to consider when building trading strategies are technical analysis (TA), fundamental analysis (FA), and EngineeringRobo.

If you would like to devise your own trading strategy, this book will help you with the basics of how you should approach speculating on the crypto markets. With a solid trading strategy, you are more likely to achieve your trading and investment goals.

WHAT IS A TRADING STRATEGY?

We can describe a trading strategy as an extensive plan for all your trading activities. It is a framework you create to guide you in all your trading endeavors.

A trading strategy can also help mitigate financial risk as it eliminates a lot of unnecessary decisions. While having a trading strategy is not mandatory for trading, it can be life-saving at times. If something unexpected happens in the market (and it will), your trading plan should define how you react – not your emotions. In other words, having a trading plan in place makes you prepared for the possible outcomes. It prevents you from making hasty, impulsive decisions that often lead to big financial losses.

For instance, a comprehensive trading strategy may include the following:

◯ What asset classes do you trade? (Cryptocurrencies, Stocks, or Commodities)

◯ How much time do you spend a day on trading? (30 minutes, 2 hours, or 6+ hours)

◯ What is your trading capital? ($1,000, $10,000, or $100,000+)

◯ What tools and indicators do you use? (Moving Average, Chart Patterns, or EngineeringRobo)

◯ What triggers your entries and exits? (Trendlines, Support & Resistance Levels, or EngineeringRobo's signals)

◯ What is your position sizing? (0.5%, 1%, or 5%)

◯ How do you measure your portfolio performance? (Daily, Weekly, or Monthly)

◯ What is your risk tolerance? (Low, Medium, or High)

WHAT TYPE OF CRYPTO TRADER ARE YOU?

Perhaps the most important change is that the world has become much more short-term oriented. All sorts of people who used to be investors are now traders. In the 1990s and 2000s, the heroes were the long-term investors; today, the heroes are the wise traders. Trading created one of the best ways to become wealthy in this decade. Why?

Your race does not matter. Your skin color does not matter. Your education does not matter, whether you are a Ph.D. or a college drop out. Your sex does not matter. Your origin does not matter. Your age does not matter. Your background and history do not matter. Your language does not matter. Your look does not matter. And your social status does not matter as long as you have sufficient funds to trade. You do not have to hire any employees. You do not have to buy or rent expensive office space. I could go on and on, but I think you get the picture.

The most important thing is to decide your trading style first. For example, when you start playing soccer, you choose your position as a goalkeeper, defender, midfielder, or forward, which will depend on your skills and interest. An easy way to figure out what you like the most in the field is by studying the techniques of your favourite players. In trading, just like in soccer, there are four styles: Scalper, Day, Swing and Position, and most successful traders tend to identify and stick to a single approach rather than mixing them up. However, there is also a fair amount of crossover between the four, at least when it comes to using technical indicators like EngineeringRobo signals. Also, if you are new to trading, it is important to look at what each approach entails to see how it suits your lifestyle!

1. **Scalping – Futures Market**
   Best Time Frame for Candlesticks: 15 minutes, 45 minutes, 3 hours
   Goal: Casual Money

Scalping is one of the quickest trading strategies out there. Scalpers do not try to take advantage of big moves or drawn-out trends. It is a strategy that focuses on exploiting small moves over and over again. For example, profiting off of bid-ask spreads, gaps in liquidity, or other inefficiencies in the market.

Scalpers do not aim to hold their positions for a long time. It is quite common to see scalp traders opening and closing positions in a matter of hours. This is why scalping is often related to High-Frequency Trading (HFT).

Scalping can be an especially lucrative strategy if a trader finds a market inefficiency that happens over and over again, and that they can exploit. Each time it happens, they can make small profits that add up over time. Scalping is generally ideal for markets with higher liquidity, where getting in and out of positions is relatively smooth and predictable.

Scalping is an advanced trading strategy that is not recommended for beginner traders due to its complexity. It also requires a deep understanding of the mechanics of the markets. The scalpers can set stop losses. While there is a risk of a stop being executed at an unfavorable price, it beats the constant monitoring of all open positions that are a feature of day trading.

2. **Day Trading – Spot & Futures Market**
   Best Time Frame for Candlesticks: 15 minutes, 45 minutes, 3 hours
   Goal: To cover the cost of living

Day trading might be the most well-known active trading strategy. People start day trading with dreams of becoming rich overnight. I am not going to say that it is impossible (because it is possible) but let me remind you that it is also very rare. Day trading is a full-time job like an engineer or a lawyer.

It's a common misconception to think that all active traders are by definition day traders, but that is not true. Day trading involves entering and exiting positions on the same day, and no position is held overnight. As such, day traders aim to capitalize on intraday price movements, i.e., price moves that happen within one trading day.

Most digital currency trading platforms are open 24 hours a day, 365 days a year. So, day trading is used in a slightly different context when it comes to the crypto markets. It typically refers to a short-term trading style, where traders enter and exit positions in a time span of 24 hours or less. Day traders will typically use price action, technical analysis and EngineeringRobo to formulate trade ideas.

Day traders typically spend more than 6 hours each day watching trade setups and short-term price movements. They use advanced charting systems which are plotted at 15- or 45-minute intervals. Day traders set a weekly target for themself. If they do achieve their weekly profit goal on the first trade Monday morning, what's next? They stop trading for that week. It does not get any better than that. Remember, they need to stick to their trading plan and their weekly goal. They do not enter into another trade once they've already achieved their weekly goal.

3. **Swing Trading – Spot Market**
   Best Time Frame for Candlesticks: 3 hours, 1 day
   Goal: 1 to 2 years. (To buy a new car? Freedom to choose what, when, and who you do things with?)

Before you trade as a swing trader, really think about what you hope to achieve. Knowing what your goal is will help you stay motivated when you are facing a tough spell of trading, and it will help you make smarter trade decisions along the way.

Swing trading relates to a style of trading that uses technical analysis as its basis. Unlike day trading, swing traders are happy to run their positions overnight and can hold for weeks if that is what their preferred technical indicators and EngineeringRobo signals are telling them to do. In this way, they hope to capture bigger moves than those expected by day traders, and this also means that they are generally prepared to take a larger risk in the hope of capturing a bigger percentage return.

Swing trading might be the most convenient active trading strategy for beginners. Capturing the "swing" of the market is the main motive here, so traders usually:

- Buy at support and sell at resistance
- Trade the bounce of the moving average
- Trade break-outs and pull-outs
- Watch closely EngineeringRobo signals

Since swing trading is seldom a full-time job, there is much less chance of burnout due to stress. Swing traders usually have a regular job or another source of income from which they can offset or mitigate trading losses.

Swing traders typically spend between 30 minutes and 4 hours each day watching trade setups and mid-term price movements. They use charting systems which are plotted by 3H, 1D, and 1W intervals.

4. Position Trading – Spot Market

Best Time Frame for Candlesticks: 1 day, 1 week
Goal: long-term 3 to 5 years (To finance a college education for your kids? To invest in a bigger house?)

Sometimes also referred to as trend trading, position trading is a strategy that involves holding positions for a longer period of time, typically at least a few months. As the name would suggest, position traders try to take advantage of directional trends. Position traders may enter a long position in an uptrend and a short position in a downtrend.

Position traders are concerned with long-term outcomes. Daily price movements and short-term market corrections, which can reverse price trends, do not affect trading decisions. Such traders allow their positions to fluctuate in sync with the general market trends over the short term.

They follow long-term historical price trends to evaluate which assets would give them the preferred financial outcome. They also use technical analysis tools and EngineeringRobo to find the right entry and exit points. In addition to that, technical tools allow them to identify long-lasting trends and potential points of reversal.

WHICH IS BETTER FOR ME?

Neither strategy is better than the other, and traders should choose the approach that works best for their skills, preferences, and lifestyle. Day trading and swing trading each have advantages and drawbacks.

It is a good idea to first decide on whether you prefer short or long-term goals before choosing a trading strategy. For instance, if you are looking to build towards your retirement years, you might favour position trading, since it gives you sufficient time to achieve your investment goals, without needing to take on riskier short-term positions.

For professional traders, swing trading is more viable than position trading, since the latter offers fewer chances of gains. The market condition has to be studied as well. If the market is showing a full-blown bullish trend, taking on a long-term position could be risky. The bullish trend will end at some point, and the market corrections could eat away at the profits made when the asset was purchased.

To find out what is really working and what is not, you should follow and track each trading strategy – without breaking the rules you set. It is also helpful to create a trading journal or sheet so you can analyze each strategy's performance.

But it is worth noting that you do not have to follow the same strategies forever. With enough data and trading records, you should be able to adjust and adapt your methods. In other words, your trading strategies should be constantly evolving as you gain trading experience.

Last but not least, you should also customize your EngineeringRobo signals depending on your trading strategy.

	Scalping	Day Trading	Swing Trading	Position Trading
Trading Analysis (Results)	Daily	Weekly	Monthly	Quarterly
Trading Time	Open to close your position	6 to 12 hours per day 5 days in a week	30 minutes to 4 hours per day	30 minutes to 4 hours per week
Typical Holding Time	Minutes to Hours	Less than 24 hours	Days to weeks	Months to up to a year
Chart interval Analysis	15 Minutes - 3H Candlesticks	15 Minutes - 3H Candlesticks	1D Daily Candlesticks 1W candlesticks for stock market	1D Daily & 1W Weekly Candlesticks
Expected Returns in % per trade	Between 1% and 20% Leverage : 5x - 20x	Between 5% and 20% Leverage : 3x - 10x	Between 20% and 100%	50% and higher
High - Priority Tips	● All the time follow EngineeringRobo's Portfolio Management ● Don't use more than 3 Robots at the same time ● Your stake size should not be more than 1% - 5% of your capital on any single trade. ● Dont use below 15M candlestick on any charts while using EngineeringRobo signals ● Never Miss The Opportunity, if you can catch 3 Buy / Sell signals in a row!			
Target Profit	Not applicable	To cover the cost of living	5% - 25% Profit per month	10% - 25% Profit per quarter

DAY TRADING VS SCALPING VS SWING TRADING

Traders should choose the strategy that complements their skills, preferences, and lifestyle as each method of trading is different.

☞ **Day Trading – Spot and Futures Market**

1. Make multiple trades per day on 15M, 45M and 3H candlesticks.

2. Positions last from minutes to the end of the working day.

3. A full-time job (6 to 12 hours a day 5 days per week). You must set a daily loss limit.

4. Multiple, smaller gains or losses. Apply a three-strike rule (maximum of three losing trades in any single day).

5. Use average 10X leverage (5x is optimal).

6. Never keep open positions while sleeping.

7. Works best in any market conditions.

☞ **Swing Trading – Spot Market**

1. Make several trades per month on 1D and 3H candlesticks.

2. Positions last from days to weeks.

3. Put 30 minutes to 4 hours per day into charting.

4. Build the portfolio depending on EngineeringRobo crypto management tool (Page #94).

5. Never keep more than 10% of the total portfolio in any of the altcoins.

6. Never keep more than 30 cryptocurrencies at the same time (maximum 20 cryptocurrencies for beginners).

7. Works best in bull market conditions.

👉 Scalping - Futures Market

1. Make multiple trades per day on 15M, 45M and 3H candlesticks. Never trade below 15M candlesticks.

2. Positions last from minutes to days, average 2 hours per day into charting is mandatory.

3. Strongly recommended being in front of the screen while having an open position (Pre- Stop loss orders & Pre- Take Profit orders could be used depending on the conditions - It is an advanced level).

4. Multiple, smaller gains or losses. Think twice about short selling.

5. Use average 10X leverage (5X for beginners).

6. Only invest between 0.5% and 1% of the total portfolio per trade.

7. Works best in bear market conditions.

🎯 **Pro-Tip:** The lower the time frame, the longer the screentime. The longer the screentime and higher the trading frequency, the greater the chances of making mistakes. I would say that the daily time frame is the smartest choice for over 50% of crypto traders. It's more significant and reliable than other timeframes.

THE UPS AND DOWNS OF TRADING CRYPTOCURRENCIES

I love the thrill of the hunt trying to find tradable cryptocurrencies. And I like having the ability to determine how much I get paid on a given day by the decisions I make. As a result, I look forward to getting up in the morning on trading days.

If you have been trading for any period of time and you do not feel this way, then this is not the career for you. And that is okay. We certainly could not have a country of people just trading cryptocurrencies. We need engineers, doctors, lawyers, school teachers, and so forth. And while I am not sure that anyone should spend 6 to 12 hours a day doing something they hate for a paycheck, this is certainly the case for traders because, after all, there is no paycheck; at least, not a guaranteed paycheck.

There are many days when I work all day with nothing to show for my efforts. In fact, being a trader is one of the few professions in which you can work hard all day and come home with less money than when you started the day. Doing this job just for the money is a surefire recipe for disappointment on all fronts. After all, you probably will not make much of a professional trader unless you love it. That is the case with any profession. The most successful people are those who have passion for what they do. You need passion to get up when many people are still asleep and search the market for potential cryptos to trade. You need passion to follow several different cryptos at a time. You need passion to bounce back after a losing day.

And even if you are that rare breed of person who can excel at doing something you hate, I have to ask, "Why?" And no, "the money" is not an acceptable first answer. There are countless ways to make money. Why choose a way that makes you (and likely) miserable? Well, the answer is financial freedom and managing your own time.

The second reason is money. Now, I know that you would not expect to read that phrase from someone who makes a living in the market, but it is true. Sure, I like money. I think it is a good thing. It is necessary for many of the necessities of life—a home, a car, food, utilities, you name it. Money pales in comparison to some of the really important things in life. I would not trade my friends for any amount of money. The same is true for my family, my parents. And certainly, the same is true for you.

There are some things that money cannot buy in your life. If that's true, then you certainly do not want to sell your actual life for money. You do not want to spend the vast majority of your waking hours doing something that you do not love just for the money. As I see it, when it quits being fun, you should quit. Now, of course, even if you absolutely love trading, you run the risk of burning out from time to time. That is why it is so important to take time off and relax or go on vacation. Take a vacation with your family, go hiking in the mountains, or just spend some time with a good book in your living room. The important thing is to get away from your computer for a while. These hiatuses from trading will not only prevent burnout, but they will make you more profitable in the long run.

Return of Cost Averaging with USD since...

	2022	2021	2020	2019	2018	2017
Bitcoin - BTC	-33,9%	-48,7%	-7,9%	37,2%	59,9%	175,6%
Ethereum - ETH	-28,8%	-38,1%	113,3%	249,2%	263,5%	671,2%
BNB - BNB	-8,1%	16,6%	482,2%	797,0%	1.196,7%	
XRP - XRP	-16,9%	-30,9%	2,4%	9,6%	2,8%	267,6%
Dogecoin - DOGE	14,4%	33,6%	1.285,6%	1.957,0%	2.096,5%	4.645,9%
Cardano - ADA	-43,1%	-57,4%	92,5%	203,7%	202,6%	
Polygon - MATIC	-0,4%	164,9%	1.833,9%			
Litecoin - LTC	10,9%	-23,1%	2,6%	10,3%	10,2%	102,7%
TRON - TRX	-17,0%	-19,2%	50,2%	76,5%	76,5%	
Chainlink - LINK	-21,0%	-47,2%	-15,7%	161,5%	523,7%	
Cosmos Hub - ATOM	-26,3%	-33,0%	39,1%			
Ethereum Classic - ETC	-23,7%	-20,6%	60,7%	114,8%	104,3%	151,5%
Monero - XMR	-10,2%	-24,7%	14,7%	44,3%	38,7%	93,5%
Stellar - XLM	-36,4%	-56,1%	-30,2%	-20,7%	-29,5%	204,7%
Bitcoin Cash - BCH	-30,7%	-56,3%	-56,5%	-54,8%	-59,3%	

Dollar-cost averaging (DCA) is a strategy where an investor invests a total sum of money in small increments over time instead of all at once. The goal is to take advantage of market downturns without risking too much capital at any given time. However, as you can see on the chart, it is not the most effective method of investing in cryptocurrencies.

AVERAGING DOWN: A TRADING STRATEGY TO AVOID OR EMBRACE?

Avoid the oldest trick in the book called dollar cost averaging. Dollar-cost averaging down is the process of buying additional crypto after you have taken a prior loss. The rationale for doing so is that now that the price has been decreased you can buy more of it and therefore increase your chances of making a profit (or at least breaking even).

Since 2016, I have read over 80 trading books, and 1,500 trading articles, I met over 50 successful day traders with over 20 years of experience. None of them are recommending "Averaging down", especially in the crypto market except Bitcoin.

Check out the link, https://whyshouldibuycrypto.com to calculate your dollar cost averaging return.

Averaging down is one of the WORST TRADING strategies that you can take or give to someone else. One of the most suicidal things that you can do in trading is to keep adding to a losing position. (Corollary: you are a poor trader if you refuse to "average down" when the fundamental and technical scenarios make such a move favorable.)

Let me give you a realistic example:

👉 **Averaging Down**	👉 **Averaging Up**
ABC coin is at $100 in January, 2022.	XYZ coin is at $10 in January, 2022.
You bought at $100 in January, it dropped.	You bought at $10 in January, it went up.
You bought at $75 in March, it dropped.	You bought at $20 in March, it went up.
You bought at $50 in July, it dropped.	You bought at $30 in July, it went up.
You bought at $10 in September, it dropped.	You bought at $45 in September, it went up.
The last ABC coin value is $5 in December.	The last XYZ coin value is $75 in December.
→ It means that you are down around 90%	→ It means that you are up around 200%
👉 You cannot sell anytime.	👉 You can sell anytime.

Most crypto investors generally believe it is a good idea to buy crypto at a lower price, in order to increase their position and potentially make a larger profit when the crypto price recovers. This strategy may work in certain cases, but more often than not you end up holding a large amount of cryptocurrencies in a failed project.

Smart Investors like to average up because they view the price increase as validation of their original thesis.

HOW TO CALCULATE POSITION SIZE IN TRADING?

No matter how big your portfolio is, you'll need to exercise proper risk management. Otherwise, you may quickly blow up your account and suffer considerable losses. Weeks or even months of progress can be wiped out by a single poorly managed trade.

The 1% rule

In the traditional financial world, there's an investing strategy called the 1% rule. According to this rule, a trader shouldn't risk more than 1% of their account on a single trade. We'll go over what that means exactly, but first, let's adjust it to be more suitable for the volatile cryptocurrency markets.

The 1% trading rule (or 1% risk rule) is a method traders use to limit their losses to a maximum of 1% of their trading capital per trade. This means they can either trade with 1% of their portfolio per trade or with a bigger order with a stop-loss equal to 1% of their portfolio value. The 1% trading rule is commonly used by day traders and scalpers but can also be adopted by swing traders.

While 1% is a general rule of thumb, some traders adjust this value according to other factors, such as account size and individual risk appetite. For instance, someone with a larger account and conservative risk appetite may choose to restrict their risk per trade to an even smaller percentage.

Risk-reward ratio

The risk-reward ratio calculates the risk that a trader will be taking relative to the potential reward. To calculate the risk-reward ratio of a trade you're considering, simply divide the potential loss by the potential profit. So, if your stop-loss is at 5% and your target is at 15% profit, your risk-reward ratio would be 1:3, meaning that the potential profit is three times higher than the risk.

How to calculate position size

Now we have all the ingredients we need to calculate position size. Let's say we have a $10,000 account. We've established that we're not risking more than 1% on a single trade. This means that we can't lose more than $100 on a single trade.

Let's say we've done our analysis of the market and have determined that our trade idea is invalidated 10% from our initial entry. In effect, when the market goes against us by 10%, we exit the trade and take the $100 loss. In other words, 10% of our position should be 1% of our account.

Account size is $10,000, account risk is 1% (0.01) and invalidation point (distance to stop-loss) is 10% (0.1)

☞ The formula to calculate position size is as follows:

Position size = account size x account risk / invalidation point, the position size will be $1,000.

WHAT ARE THE FUTURES TRADING RULES YOU LIVE BY?

1. Do not open a long position at the resistance level.

2. Do not open a short position at the support level.

3. Do not keep more than 7 different long positions or short positions at the same time.

4. Do not keep your loss position open for a long time while EngineeringRobo signals are against your trade.

5. If you have $10,000 in your total trading account, you should transfer around $3,000 into futures account.

Out of the $3,000 futures account, each of your position should be only $30 (1% rule).

6. If you are in the first 3-6 months of the learning process, do not use more than 10x leverage (5x is ideal).

7. If EngineeringRobo is bullish on the coin on both 1D, 3H and 45M candlesticks do not open a short position.

8. If EngineeringRobo is bearish to the coin on both 1D, 3H and 45M candlesticks do not open a long position.

9. 45 Minutes and 3H are the best time frames to open a short or long position.

10. Never keep a long position or short position when you go to sleep, if you do, you should put a stop-loss order.

11. Mainly trade on 3H but do not ignore major support and resistance on 1D time frame (Orange Horizontal Lines).

12. If EngineeringRobo is not bearish on both 1D and 3H but you really want to open a short position, make sure that the candles are at around the resistance level.

13. If EngineeringRobo is not bullish on both 1D and 3H but you really want to open a long position, make sure that the candles are at around the support level.

14. The key to making money in the futures markets is in how you exit the market (You can enter the market randomly and still make money).

15. Shorting is about three times as hard as longing cryptocurrencies.

→ Keep your position until 3H signals turn against your trade position.

→ Take 50% of your money back when you double your money.

🎯 **Pro-tip:** If you are opening max 7 positions at the same time, one or two of them should be an opposite trade (5 long - 2 short, 5 short - 2 long).

WHAT ADVICE WOULD YOU GIVE TO NOVICE TRADERS?

A very small percentage of traders "make it". If you have an intense desire to be successful and are willing to study, learn from professional traders, and correct mistakes, you can make it too. You're a human which means you can learn a lot about markets by simply observing your own behavior and emotions.

My philosophy is that all cryptos are bad as a trader. There are no good cryptos unless they go up in price. If they go down instead, you have to cut your losses fast. The secret to winning in the crypto market does not include being right all the time. In fact, you should be able to win even if you are right only half the time. The key is to lose the least amount of money possible when you are wrong.

1. If you don't work very hard, it is extremely unlikely that you will be a great trader.
2. It takes 1,000 trades to learn how to trade. If you try to learn from every single trade that you make, you are only going to get better and better as time goes on.
3. Successful traders spend no more than 20 percent of their time trading, but 80 percent of their time studying and improving their techniques.
4. The markets trend only about 20 percent of the time; the rest of the time they move sideways.
5. If you have a loss on a trade after a month or two, you are clearly wrong. Even when you are around breakeven, but a significant amount of time has passed, you are probably wrong here too.
6. If you have a losing position that is making you uncomfortable, the solution is very simple: Get out, because you can always get back in.

7. If you own a portfolio of crypto, you must learn to sell the worst performers first and keep the best a little longer. In other words, always sell your mistakes while the loss is still small, and watch your better trades to see if they progress into your big winners.
8. Every 50 percent loss began as a 10 percent or 20 percent loss. Learn to always sell coins quickly when you have a small loss rather than waiting and hoping they'll come back.
9. Buy coins as much as you can track easily. If you are comfortable tracking 10 coins, then you should buy a max of 10 coins not more!
10. Remember, you don't always have to trade in every situation. In fact, if you have been playing your cash account the right way, both defensively and offensively, you can choose to sit out trading days when it is not clear you will make a profit.
11. Using too much leverage will destroy you. When things are going well, it's amazing. But the geometric series swings both ways and markets usually move downward faster than upward.
12. I would advise always use stops when you go to sleep while trading on futures market. I mean actually put them in because that commits you to get out at a certain point. Place your stops at a point that, if reached, will reasonably indicate that the trade is wrong,' not at a point determined primarily by the maximum dollar amount you are willing to lose per contract. You can also use a time stop. If you think a market should break, and it doesn't, you can get out even if you are not losing any money.
13. Expect failure! How do you respond to trading adversity? Do you ask poor trading questions? Asking quality questions and getting answers can move you closer to your trading goals.
14. I would say always bet 1 percent of your money on any one idea. That way you can be wrong a hundred times; it will take you a long time to lose your money.

15. You can risk 1 percent of your capital as a scalper, you can risk 5 percent as a swing trader, or you can risk 10 percent as a position trader, but you must realize that the more you risk, the more volatile the results are going to be.
16. Selling short is quite tricky. Short selling of individual cryptos should only be considered after both the EngineeringRobo gave sell signals and the candles are dropping from the resistance level.
17. Make it a rule never to lose more than a certain amount like a maximum of 20 percent on any crypto you buy. If crypto drops 20 percent below your purchase price, you will automatically sell it at the market—no second-guessing, no hesitation. EngineeringRobo also gives sell signals at around 20% loss in most of conditions.
18. Generally, the daily and weekly time frame is used to establish a longer-term trend, whereas shorter time frames like 3-hour chart time frame is used to spot ideal entries into the market.
19. Find a mentor as soon as possible to reach your trading goals easily.

PART III

HOW TO GET THE MAXIMUM RETURNS FROM CRYPTO MARKET CYCLES?	52
WHAT IS THE BEST TIMEFRAME TO TRADE CRYPTO?	54
LEVERAGE IN CRYPTO MARKET: A DOUBLE-EDGED SWORD	56
HIGH LEVERAGE RISKS AND BENEFITS	58
HOW TO TRADE LIKE A HEDGE FUND TRADER IN CRYPTO?	60
WHAT IS TECHNICAL ANALYSIS?	64

HOW TO GET THE MAXIMUM RETURNS FROM CRYPTO MARKET CYCLES?

⚠️ Keep 2 or 3 different portfolios in bull markets.

⚠️ Keep 3 different portfolios in bear markets.

Investment Portfolio Account: It covers between 20% and 30% of your all-crypto net-worth.

1. Long Term portfolio.

2. You completed deep research about all the coins that you hold in your investment portfolio.

3. You do adjust your investment portfolio once every 6 months.

4. You set target levels in advance to sell cryptos " before" you buy.

Example- 1; you bought XRP at $0.25, and you set the plan to hold until XRP reaches $1.

Example- 2; you bought ETH at $1,000, and you set the plan to hold until ETH reaches $2,000.

5. No need to hold USDT in this account unless you are staking your USDT.

Swing Portfolio Account: It covers between 50% and 60% of your all-crypto net-worth.

1. Middle Term Portfolio.

2. You adjust your swing portfolio depending on EngineeringRobo's crypto portfolio management tool.

3. You build your trading strategy on 1D timeframe.

4. You follow EngineeringRobo's signals on 1D timeframe.

5. If both the chart patterns and EngineeringRobo are bullish, you can buy it. You don't need to deep research crypto projects.

6. None of the altcoins should cover more than 10% of your total swing portfolio.

7. You must hold between 10% and 70% of your portfolio in USDT depending on EngineeringRobo's crypto swing portfolio management tool.

Futures Market / Scalping Portfolio: It covers between 10% and 30% of your all-crypto net-worth.

1. Short Term Portfolio.

2. This scalping portfolio is a must portfolio to make money during the bear markets.

3. You trade on 15M, 45M or 3H timeframe with EngineeringRobo signals.

4. You trade on futures market.

5. You should bet a maximum of 1% of your futures trading portfolio per trade.

6. You shouldn't use more than 20X leverage.

7. Never keep a long / short position when you go to sleep if you do, you should put a stop-loss order.

WHAT IS THE BEST TIMEFRAME TO TRADE CRYPTO?

Some traders hold positions in the market for hours. While others hold them for weeks, months or even years.

So, who's right? And which approach should you use?

New crypto traders want to get rich quickly so they start trading small time frames like the 15-minute or 45-minute charts. Then they end up getting frustrated when they trade because the time frame doesn't fit their trading style.

The smaller the time frame, the more EngineeringRobo signals there will be. But getting a lot of buying signals or selling signals isn't necessarily a good thing if you do not know how to deal with so many signals.

👉 15 Minutes – 45 Minutes timeframe

1. Short-term trading demands a lot of your time per day.

2. Highest focus required.

3. More opportunities for trades, and many signals.

4. Target 1% - 5% return per trade.

5. Risk only 1% or 0.5% of the account on a trade.

👉 45 Minutes - 3 Hours timeframe

1. A daily commitment of at least two hours.

2. Requires sharp focus.

3. Excellent time frame for day traders and scalpers.

4. Target 5% - 20% return per trade.

5. Risk 1% of the account on a trade.

👉 3 Hours - 1 Day timeframe

1. Demands between 30 minutes and 4 hours per day in front of the computer.

2. Fewer trades per month and more time to think through each trade.

3. The best timeframe for swing trading is daily timeframes. And while it's possible to swing trade in other timeframes, the daily timeframe holds some quite big advantages that make it a good choice.

4. Target 20% - 100% return per trade.

5. Risk between 1% and 5% of the account on a trade.

Using several timeframes allow you to see the whole picture. This is called "multiple timeframe analysis". Multi-timeframe analysis can help you make better decisions. Rule of three is an unwritten rule that recommends that a scalper should use three timeframes before they initiate a trade. (1D – 3H – 45M). The rule of three is an essential trading strategy since it can help you avoid making simple mistakes like entering a short trade on 45-Minute when an asset has just moved above a key support level on daily.

LEVERAGE IN CRYPTO MARKET: A DOUBLE-EDGED SWORD

Leverage is the use of borrowed funds to increase one's trading position beyond what would be available from their cash balance alone. Knowing the different leverage amounts, as well as their weaknesses and strengths, will definitely help you choose the right one for your trading. And picking the right leverage is one of the most important steps in being sure you have the right tools to trade – ones that fit your trading personality, goals, and the amount of time you can dedicate to trading. One is not better than another.

Rule 1: Determine Engineering Robo signals

Rule 2: Determine Timeframes

Rule 3: Determine Leverage Amount

Rule 4: Determine Entry and Exit

☞ 1X - 3X Leverage

1. Ideal for swing traders.

2. Beginners: 1- 3 months in futures market.

3. Maximum 5% stake per trade.

4. Follow EngineeringRobo signals on 1D timeframe.

☞ 3X - 10X Leverage

1. More appropriate for day traders and scalpers.

2. Intermediate: 3- 12 months in futures market.

3. Average 1% stake per trade.

4. Follow EngineeringRobo signals on 3H timeframe.

👉 10X - 20X Leverage

1. Ideal for day traders and scalpers.

2. Advanced: 12+ months in futures market.

3. Maximum 1% stake per trade.

4. Follow EngineeringRobo Signals on 45-Minute and 3H timeframes.

👉 20X - 50X Leverage

1. Risky for scalpers.

2. Master: 24+ months in futures market.

3. Maximum 0.5% or 1% stake per trade.

4. Follow EngineeringRobo signals on 15-Minute and 45-Minute timeframes.

👁 Trading with too high a leverage amount is one of the most common errors made by new crypto traders. Until you become more experienced, I strongly recommend that you trade with a lower amount. You can choose any leverage amount but hopefully this book has given you the information to choose your leverage more wisely.

YOUR INVESTMENT   LEVERAGE   YOUR TRADING POWER

HIGH LEVERAGE RISKS AND BENEFITS

Debt is bad, as we've all heard. However, this is not always the case. Debt can be used to build credit, start building equity through the purchase of a new home, or even leverage it to make a profit-generating investment. Debt can also be referred to as leverage.

So, what is exactly leverage? Leverage is the ability to control or manage a large sum of money using a small amount of your own money and borrowing the rest. In financial lingo, this is known as Other People's Money (OPM).

A good example of leverage at work is when an investor borrows money to invest in a crypto. Let's say, the price of Ethereum is trading at $2,000 and you have $10,000, without leverage; the maximum number of crypto you can buy is 5. If the Ethereum's price rises to $4,000 and you decide to exit, your maximum profit will be $10,000. However, if you go to a bank and borrow $10,000 extra and use it to buy Ethereum, you can now afford to buy 10. When the Ethereum doubles, your total will be $40,000. After returning the borrowed funds to the bank, your profit will be $30,000 minus the crypto exchange's interest.

When leverage works, it is very useful to traders and investors. When it fails, the losses can exceed the initial capital of the investor leading to negative balances. In the example above, if the crypto fell to zero, the investor would first suffer a personal loss of $10,000. They would then need $10,000 more to pay back to the crypto exchange.

You must clearly understand that you will be in such a difficult situation if your trading plan doesn't go as you think. Not only does leverage amplify your losses, but it also amplifies your transaction costs. The associated transaction costs of using high leverage can gradually drain your capital.

Let's say you have deposited 10,000 USDT in your futures wallet. You decided to open a 20x leverage position with your 10,000 USDT deposit, giving you a total exposure of 200,000 USDT (10,000 x 20). Considering the standard crypto exchange taker fee of 0.04%, the cost to open this position will be 80 USDT — that is 0.8% of your account!

With one trade and the market not even moving yet, you already have to account for a 0.8% loss from your overall P&L. Therefore, your account balance shrinks if your position goes wrong, thereby increasing your effective leverage. Furthermore, when trading perpetual contracts, you would incur funding fees that are charged every eight hours. Assuming a low funding fee of 0.01% (or 0.04% daily), this would translate to an additional 80 USDT daily deduction from your account balance.

Therefore, traders must consider the associated cost of using high leverage as it may have a profound impact on your account over time: the higher your leverage, the higher your transaction cost as a percentage of your trading capital.

- While leverage has a lot of upside potential, it can also end up costing you a lot more than you borrowed, especially if you can't keep up with interest payments. This is especially true if you invest money that isn't your own. Leverage, at least when it comes to investing, should be reserved for seasoned pros until you have experience—and can afford to lose money.

HOW TO TRADE LIKE A HEDGE FUND TRADER IN CRYPTO?

After having over six years of financial market experience, I have realized that all pro traders and money managers work in a similar way. In fact, some of the world's very best traders use technical analysis, the most famous include Jim Simons, Paul Tudor Jones, and Stanley Druckenmiller.

Their strategies may be different, but the way they come about developing these strategies is not. The difference between a professional and an unprofessional trader is that a professional never goes into a trade blindly. This is an important because in order for professional money managers to be confident enough to solicit investments into their funds, not only do they need to have a battle-tested strategy, but they also need to know when the fund succeeds, when it fails, and how bad things can get.

As retail or individual traders, our $10,000 accounts are just as important as any $10 million hedge fund. In fact, our accounts may be even more important, because we are trading with our own money whereas the $10 million hedge fund trader is most likely trading with other people's money. Therefore, if all hedge fund traders follow a four-step process in developing their trading strategies, there is no reason why individual traders should not do so as well.

The best way to develop a trading strategy is to follow a four-step top-down approach:

1. Properly defining the trading style

Every hedge fund trader, like every trader, follows a different methodology. Some will only use chart pattern analysis, while others will only use robo advisors like EngineeringRobo. The first thing to do is to figure out what type of trader you are and what type of style you want to trade in.

2. The art of entering and exiting

When hedge fund traders design trading strategies, they give a great deal of thought to both entries and exits. There are primarily two different ways to enter or exit a trade:

A. Single entry, single exit: With a single entry and a single exit, traders simply place their entire position at one price and then sell their entire position at another price.

B. Multiple entries, multiple exits: With multiple entries and multiple exits, traders scale both into and out of their positions. This is a tactic frequently used by trend traders. They average up into a position by adding to winning trades and scale out of the position to capitalize on as much of the trend as possible. With automatic systems, entry and exit strategies are set in stone and coded into the system. Traders should try to approach entries and exits in the same way by deciding which of the four combinations to use before laying on a trade.

3. Test drive

You will never buy a car without test-driving it, so you should never trade a strategy without back-testing it! For hedge fund traders and traders of automated trading systems, back-testing is extremely important because if a trading strategy did not make money in the past, how can they believe that the strategy will make money in the future?

For example, open your chart, activate EngineeringRobo, and look for a minimum of 50 examples of the strategy working. Then downgrade the time frame of your charts to make sure that the strategy could have been executed at your desired price.

4. Work hard at learning how to trade properly

If you ever have the privilege to ask questions to successful hedge fund traders you'll realize just how much effort, time, determination, and lost money it took until they arrived at where they are. Being a consistent crypto market winner is no different from being a top lawyer, doctor or businessman.

PART IV

WHAT IS TECHNICAL ANALYSIS?	64
4 EASY STEPS TO BE A MASTER AT TECHNICAL ANALYSIS	65
CHART PATTERNS CHEAT SHEET	67
BUY AT THE SUPPORT AND SELL AT THE RESISTANCE	69
FIBONACCI LEVELS	70
MOVING AVERAGE TRADING SECRETS	70
SO WHY DO PEOPLE USE MOVING AVERAGES?	71

WHAT IS TECHNICAL ANALYSIS?

Technical analysis (TA), often referred to as charting, is a type of analysis that aims to predict future market behavior based on previous price action and volume data. The TA approach is extensively applied to stocks and other assets in traditional financial markets, but it is also an integral component of trading digital currencies in the cryptocurrency market.

In contrast to fundamental analysis (FA), which considers multiple factors around the price of an asset, TA is strictly focused on historical price action. Therefore, it is utilized as a tool to examine an asset's price fluctuations and volume data, and many traders employ it in an attempt to identify trends and favorable trading opportunities.

While primitive forms of technical analysis appeared in the 17th-century Amsterdam and 18th-century Japan, the modern TA is often traced back to the work of Charles Dow. A financial journalist and founder of The Wall Street Journal, Dow was among the first to observe that individual assets and markets often move in trends that could be segmented and examined. His work later gave birth to the Dow Theory which encouraged further developments in technical analysis.

In the early stages, the rudimentary approach of technical analysis was based on hand-made sheets and manual calculations, but with the advance of technology and modern computing, TA became widespread and is now an important tool for many investors and traders. However, drawing trend lines is still an art. It's ok — Not everyone can be great at it.

4 EASY STEPS TO BE A MASTER AT TECHNICAL ANALYSIS

Only about 15 to 20 percent of traders really understand the real power of technical charts. Even a lot of professionals are totally ignorant about charts. Just as a doctor would be foolish not to use X-rays, traders would be foolish not to use charts. Charts provide valuable information about what is going on that cannot be obtained easily in any other way.

1. You should always start to draw downtrend lines from the highest hill level to the second-highest hill point.

2. The line extension should go to the future - not the past dates.

3. Two hills are enough to draw the downtrend lines.

4. You don't need to hurry to buy it if the candles are still below the downtrend line.

1. You should always start to draw uptrend lines from the lowest reverse hill to the second lowest reverse hill.

2. The line extension should go to the future - not the past dates.

3. Two hills are enough to draw the uptrend lines.

4. You don't need to hurry to sell it if the candles are still above the uptrend line.

Pro-tip: No single technical approach works all the time. You have to know when to use each method.

CHART PATTERNS CHEAT SHEET

We studied 12 different patterns in crypto market for a time period of 3 years with more than 250 case studies for each and every single pattern. Here is the list of patterns that were involved in the study along with their respective success rates, as they were revealed in the 3-year study:

- Descending & Ascending Triangles: 68.75%

- Head & Shoulders Pattern: 66.62%

- Bearish & Bullish Wedges: 59.22%

- Bullish & Bearish Flags: 60.74%

- Symmetrical Triangle: 64.10%

- Double Top & Bottom Patterns: 61.28%

We received the highest success rate on Support & Resistance zone concept with 74.50%!

Do not use any of these basic patterns as a stand-alone trading technique. Instead, you should consider these patterns with EngineeringRobo signals and a solid-strong support & resistance system.

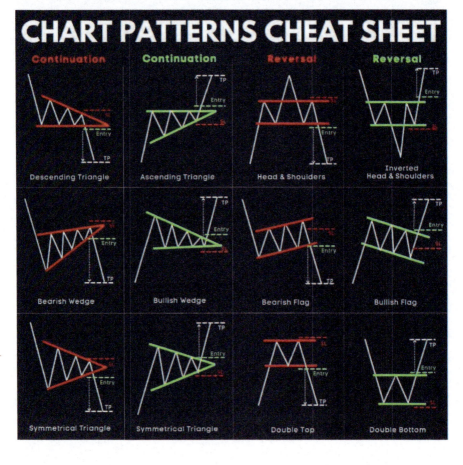

BUY AT THE SUPPORT AND SELL AT THE RESISTANCE

The concepts of support and resistance are some of the most fundamental topics related to the technical analysis of financial markets. They apply to essentially any market, whether that's stocks, forex, commodities, or cryptocurrencies.

While they're simple concepts to understand, **they're actually quite difficult to master**. Identifying them can be entirely subjective, they'll work differently in changing market conditions, and you'll need to understand the different types. But above all, you'll need to study a lot of charts, and this book will help you get started. On the most fundamental level, support and resistance are simple concepts. The price finds a level that it's unable to break through, with this level acting as a barrier of some sort. In the case of support, the price finds a "floor," while in the case of resistance, it finds a "ceiling." Basically, you could think of support as a zone of demand and resistance as a zone of supply. Only make trades when support and resistance levels reinforce that decision.

While more traditionally, support and resistance are indicated as lines, real-world cases are usually not as precise. Bear in mind; the markets aren't driven by some physical law that prevents them from breaching a specific level. This is why it may be more beneficial to think of support and resistance as areas. You can think of these areas as ranges on a price chart that will likely drive increased activity from traders.

Support and resistance are key concepts when it comes to exercising proper risk management. The ability to consistently identify these zones can present favorable trading opportunities. Typically, two things can happen once the price reaches an area of support or resistance. It either bounces away from the area or breaks through it and continues in the direction of the trend – potentially to the next support or resistance area.

FIBONACCI LEVELS

While many of the features of Fibonacci sequences appear throughout nature, investors have harnessed its power to predict crypto prices.

Levels of support and resistance – a downside to using retracements – can only be measured by looking backward. However, these reviews offer impressive patterns. For example, reviewing Bitcoin's decline from a peak of $13,895 to a low of $3926.61, we saw a strong resistance at 0.618 for a few months. Also, we completed a gap through the other strong support levels that led to the ultimate low. Applying Fibonacci levels at these events would have revealed a downside price target.

0.618 and 0.382 are the most important horizontal levels of Fibonacci (strongest lines – hard to penetrate, the trend will continue in the same direction most likely)

MOVING AVERAGE TRADING SECRETS

Moving Averages are one of the most widely used indicators in technical analysis. Whether you're a new trader or a veteran investor you should be familiar with this concept.

Moving averages represent the average price of a cryptocurrency over a specified period of time. The most commonly used periods are the 20, 50, and 200-day averages. But, depending on timeframe and style, some traders use the 20-day while longer-term investors might use the 50-day.

A 50-day moving average represents the average price of a cryptocurrency over the last 50 days. Take the sum of a crypto's closing price over a certain number of days (50, 100, etc.) and then divide that sum by the set number of days. Do that continually and you will find a crypto-moving average over time.

SO WHY DO PEOPLE USE MOVING AVERAGES?

There are several reasons like it helps traders analyze a trend. Is crypto trading above or below its moving average? How long has it been trading below or above it? The answers to these questions help some traders and investors determine the trend of crypto. They also provide unique looks at market breadth.

The moving average can be used for many tactics. Another way is to determine a stock's support and resistance levels. For example, if cryptocurrency is in a strong bullish upward trend, the 50-day moving average may serve as support. Meaning the price will test and bounce off the 50-day line on pullbacks. Some traders will stay long a stock as long as its price is above the 50-day. The second it breaks; however, they sell out.

Strategy A – The candles start from above the 200-MA line, once the candle touches the 200-MA line, buy at this point. If candles go up, enjoy the profit. If a 1D candle drops below the 200-MA line after you buy, wait until the current candle to close the next day to sell.

Strategy B – The candles start from below the 200-MA line, once the candle touches the 200-MA line, pay attention to the next candle. If the next candle is fully above the 200-MA line, buy at the following candle. If the next candle stays at the 200-MA line, just pay attention.

Strategy 1 – If 20-MA and 50-MA are crossed and the 20-MA line is going up, this is a buy signal. If 20-MA and 50-MA are crossed and the 50-MA line is going up, this is a sell signal.

Strategy 2 - If 50-MA and 200-MA are crossed and the 50-MA line is going up, this is a buy signal. If 50-MA and 200-MA are crossed and the 200-MA line is going up, this is a sell signal.

◎ **Pro-tip:** We have tested 1830 different MA and EMA combinations to find the most profitable pair from over 10 years of data across crypto and stock markets. Then, we found the best and most profitable Golden Cross and Dead Cross MA signals ever. You must try EngineeringRobo's Ultimate MA signals – UMAC.

PART V

IS ALGOTRADING THE FUTURE OF CRYPTO TRADING?	74
WHAT IS ENGINEERINGROBO?	76
WHY DO YOU NEED ENGINEERINGROBO?	77
ENGINEERINGROBO'S FORMULA	79
ROBO ADVISORS BACKTESTING	81
DON'T USE MORE THAN 3 ROBO SIGNALS AT THE SAME TIME. WHY?	85
HOW TO PICK WINNING CRYPTOCURRENCIES	87
HOW TO USE ENGINEERINGROBO ON CHARTS	89
BULL MARKET CASE STUDIES	92
BEAR MARKET CASE STUDIES	93
ENGINEERINGROBO'S CRYPTO PORTFOLIO MANAGEMENT TOOL	94
DEVELOP YOUR OWN STRATEGY IN ENGINEERINGROBO	96

IS ALGOTRADING THE FUTURE OF CRYPTO TRADING?

Algorithmic trading, or algo trading, has been around for decades and it has been one of the most effective trading strategies for traditional markets like stocks and forex. In the next decade, many studies predict that artificial intelligence and algorithmic trading will grow from under $6 billion in 2022 to over $64 billion by 2030. There are over 150 algorithmic trading robots available all over the world, and more are being developed every year.

Nowadays, algorithmic trading has also become very popular among crypto traders because of its effectiveness and flexibility in terms of risk management as well as scalability. Algorithmic trading can be useful in the fast-paced and volatile world of cryptocurrency trading for a number of reasons. For one, it can help traders execute trades more quickly and efficiently than they could manually search for potential trades on charting platforms. This can be particularly useful in a market like crypto, where prices can fluctuate rapidly and opportunistic trading opportunities can arise and disappear in a matter of hours.

Additionally, algorithmic trading can also help traders manage their risks more effectively. By using algorithms to automatically monitor and manage their positions, traders can set specific rules and parameters for their trades, such as stop-loss orders that automatically close a trade if it reaches a certain level of loss. This can help traders limit their losses and avoid making rash, emotional decisions in the heat of the moment.

Furthermore, algorithmic trading can be more objective and less prone to human error than manual trading. Because algorithms are designed to execute trades based on predetermined rules and criteria, they can avoid the biases and emotional responses that can sometimes affect human traders. This can help traders make more rational and informed decisions, potentially leading to more successful trades.

Overall, algo trading can help traders in the crypto market execute trades more efficiently, implement more sophisticated trading strategies, and manage their risks more effectively.

Things To Keep In Mind

1. Cost

Developing and maintaining an algorithmic trading system can be expensive, especially for smaller investors or traders who may not have the resources to invest in sophisticated technology.

2. Expertise in programming languages

Developing complex algorithms requires an understanding of coding languages such as C++, Java, Python, Pine script, etc. The quality of software varies from algorithm to algorithm, and utilizing a badly coded algorithm may result in financial loss. That's why you need to look for a reputable algorithmic robot with a proven track record of success.

3. Intense financial knowledge

A successful trading strategy needs to be adapted to a continuously changing financial markets. It is likely that you will lose money if you choose an algorithmic robot that is designed solely for bull markets. The key to developing an algorithmic trading system that really works is taking into account a variety of market cycles. At any given moment, a market can go from being in a bull market to being in a bear market.

4. Access to API Keys

The majority of algorithmic robots ask for API keys to manage your fund. In general, API keys are not considered secure; they are typically accessible to clients, making them easy to steal. Unless the trader revokes or regenerates the key, the stolen key can be used indefinitely.

⚠️ By using EngineeringRobo, you'll never have to provide an API key.

WHAT IS ENGINEERINGROBO?

EngineeringRobo is a robo advisor that uses a computer program that follows a defined set of instructions to create successful entry and exit ideas for traders and investors.

EngineeringRobo offers strategic trading entry and exit points, so you can preserve capital before markets tumble, and take full advantage as they start to rebound. At a glance, market timing indicators tell investors whether market conditions are right or whether it's safer on the sideline.

EngineeringRobo is tailored for people who are looking to create a new source of income from trading, looking to grow their investments, and/or looking to pursue a career in the world of finance!

WHY DO YOU NEED ENGINEERINGROBO?

In a 2003 article published in the Financial Analysts Journal titled "The Profitability of Day Traders", professors at the University of Texas found that out of 334 brokerage accounts day trading the U.S. markets between February 1998 and October 1999, only 35% were profitable and only 14% generated profits in excess of than $10,000.

In a 2005 article published in the Journal of Applied Finance titled "The Profitability of Active Stock Traders" professors at the University of Oxford and the University College Dublin found that out of 1,146 brokerage accounts day trading the U.S. markets between March 8, 2000 and June 13, 2000, only 50% were profitable with an average net profit of $16,619.

In a research paper published in 2014 titled "Do Day Traders Rationally Learn About Their Ability?", professors from the University of California studied 3.7 billion trades from the Taiwan Stock Exchange between 1992-2006 and found that only 9.81% of day trading volume was generated by predictably profitable traders and that these predictably profitable traders constitute less than 3% of all day traders on an average day.

The range of results in these three studies exemplifies the challenge of determining a definitive success rate for day traders. At a minimum, these studies indicate at least 90% of aspiring day traders will not be profitable. However, thousands of traders still enter the market every day, making the same mistakes repeatedly (due to a lack of emotional discipline)

While other traders, equipped with trading algorithms (or cold-blooded 100% emotional control) wait on the sidelines like a shark, ready to pounce on their prey and collect the profit from their mistake.

Therefore, there are only two ways to win in this game of trading:

1. Either spend over 10,000+ hours looking at the crypto charts and build the emotional training required for consistent profitability (they call it "screen time" on Wall Street)

2. Or use a trading algorithm that will filter out the bad trades for you, and show you exactly at what price to buy and at what price to sell for max profit.

And that is our goal with EngineeringRobo. Using advanced mathematical models, we remove the emotional element from trading, allowing you to trade like a robot.

In our opinion, the key to developing an algorithmic trading system that actually works is to account for multiple market conditions. By taking a market direction agnostic position, EngineeringRobo has been attempting to outperform in both bull and bear market conditions with 550+ active EngineeringRobo traders worldwide (and counting) since 2019.

ENGINEERINGROBO'S FORMULA

EngineeringRobo's unique algorithm finds profitable cryptocurrencies, stocks and commodities based on their Ichimoku, VPVR, ATR, Fibonacci Levels, Moving Averages, RSI, MACD, Stochastic, Bollinger Bands, Volumes and Price Changes to give you entry and exit ideas.

● What is a Support & Resistance indicator?

Support and Resistance areas are one of the most used techniques in technical analysis. It can be identified by pivot points. The pivot points identify supply and demand zones at specific instances and timeframes, depending on the trend, and hence known as support and resistance indicator. If the price falls below a support level, that level will become resistance. If the price rises above a resistance level, it will often become support.

● What is a VPVR indicator?

The VPVR indicator shows volume by price. In other words, VPVR shows how many transactions or trades occur at a specific price point. It is an extremely powerful tool that traders can use to help take their strategies to the next level.

● What does ATR stand for?

The average true range (ATR) is a technical analysis indicator that measures market volatility by decomposing the entire range of an asset price for that period. It is a volatility indicator that shows how much an asset moves, on average, during a given time frame. The indicator can help day traders confirm when they might want to initiate a trade, and it can be used to determine the placement of a stop-loss order.

◉ What Is a MACD indicator?

Moving Average Convergence Divergence (MACD) is a trend-following momentum indicator that shows the relationship between two moving averages of a security's price. The MACD is an extremely popular indicator used in technical analysis.

◉ What is a Stochastic oscillator?

A stochastic oscillator is a momentum indicator comparing a particular closing price of a security to a range of its prices over a certain period of time. The sensitivity of the oscillator to market movements is reducible by adjusting that time period or by taking a moving average of the result.

◉ What is a Bollinger Band?

When stock prices continually touch the upper Bollinger Band, the prices are thought to be overbought; conversely, when they continually touch the lower band, prices are thought to be oversold, triggering a buy signal.

◉ What does Golden Cross stand for?

The golden cross is a technical chart pattern indicating the potential for a major rally. The golden cross appears on a chart when a stock's short-term moving average crosses above its long-term moving average. The golden cross can be contrasted with a death cross indicating a bearish price movement.

ROBO ADVISORS BACKTESTING

Backtesting is one of the most important aspects of developing a trading system. It is the general method for seeing how well a strategy or model would have done ex-post. Backtesting assesses the viability of a trading strategy by discovering how it would play out using historical data. If created and interpreted properly, it can help traders optimize and improve their strategies, find any technical or theoretical flaws, as well as gain confidence in their strategy before applying it to real-world markets.

Backtesting can be a simple or complex process, and traders may use either automated or manual testing. The former requires automated software that searches for trades that meet the strategy criteria, then adds up the winning and losing trades to show if the strategy was profitable over a specified amount of time. Manual Backtesting refers to a process where traders analyse past trades based on their strategies, and then add up the results themselves.

Let's do some Backtesting with EngineeringRobo between 1875 and 1885 – the oldest date on the charting platform. The chart data is below almost 150 years old! Yes, EngineeringRobo also worked perfectly at that time.

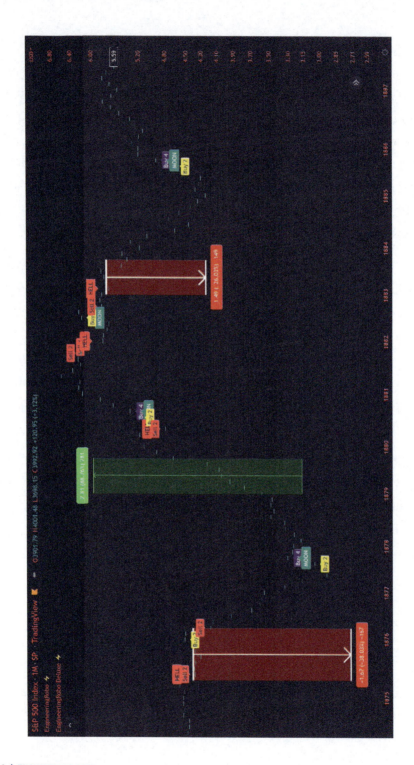

By Backtesting EngineeringRobo, at least we can ascertain how prices have reacted to similar circumstances historically, even though we know it cannot guarantee a strategy's future performance.

Algorithmic trades allow you to potentially identify and take advantage of trends while being in full control of your trades. It can take years to learn how to properly read charts, understand the different pairs to be able to successfully & consistently pick the right trades, and even then, with all the experience in the world, traders still have to spend hours and hours sitting in front of computer screens analysing the markets & news while trying to control human emotions in order to be successful.

It's actually the human emotions that are responsible for a lot of mistakes that traders make, they could have had an argument with their partner, could be stressed over bills or even something as small as a bad night's sleep can have an effect on how they trade.

You see, computers have no emotions, and it is the software that identifies patterns in the market based on historical data. It's eliminating the bad trades made on emotions such as fear, greed and excitement that is the real game changer here!

EngineeringRobo was first launched in 2019 and has since been updated into 10 different buy and sell indicators that users can add to their charts. The EngineeringRobo team is dedicated to creating profitable trading strategies for traders around the world. Some of the Backtesting results from our robo advisors below.

Somebody with a Ph.D. in statistics once told me that you need at least 50 trades in order to produce statistically relevant results. We have tested robo advisors on over 200 different conditions.

- Remember, past performance isn't a guarantee for future performance.

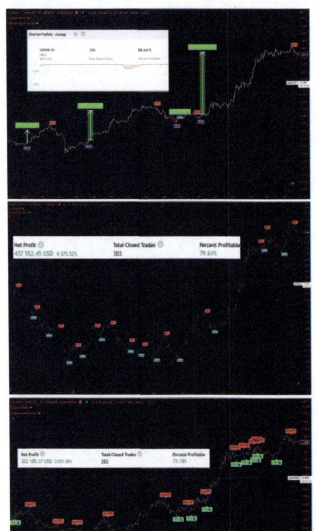

1 - Robo 4 Signals

Truly a unique tool for technical analysis as it includes calculation of specific metrics like SAR + MACD + Price Movement that gives you buy and sell signals.

🟢 Buy-4 and Sell-4 signals

2. Moon & Hell Signals

This strategy uses combined indicators to create buy and sell signals. It works perfectly in bull and bear markets.

🟢 Moon = Buy signal
🟢 Hell = Sell signal

3. Bull & Bear Signals

It is also called a Money Flow; it shows you where money goes:

To Bulls or Bears?

It might give false signals in sideways trends

🟢 Bull = Buy signal
🟢 Bear = Sell signal

DON'T USE MORE THAN 3 ROBO SIGNALS AT THE SAME TIME. WHY?

Our Backtesting results show that using three robo-advisors increased the success rate by 35 percent compared to only one robo-advisor. The average Backtesting results with three robo-advisors scored also 14 percent higher than using two robo-advisors. We received the highest success rate by using three robo-advisors.

If we pick 4 robo-advisors, we might not make any decisions if 2 robo-advisors are bullish and 2 robo-advisors are bearish. It applies for picking only 2 robo advisors or other even numbers. If you also pick too many robo-advisors, you might get confused about the signals.

For example, Robo 4 already included 3 different indicators in the formula.

Robo 4 includes the calculation of specific metrics like SAR + MACD + Price Movement that gives you Buy 4 and Sell 4 signals. If you use more than 3 robo signals, you try to use around " 10 - 12 " different indicators at the same time! The old adage "less is more" is often applicable when it comes to crypto trading with EngineeringRobo.

To get maximum results from your robo-advisors, follow the advice below;

A) 3 robo signals B) 3 robo signals + 1 side strategy

A or B + Pick one bonus below 👇

Side strategies:

👉 McGinley Dynamic   👉 EMA Trendlines   👉 20-MA & 50-MA
👉 Support and Resistance levels

Robo signals:

→ Robo 1: It is popular among Day Traders. It generates buy-1 and sell-1 signals.

→ Robo 2: It fits for all types of traders. It generates buy-2 and sell-2 signals.

→ Robo 3: The robo advisor of the bull markets. It generates buy-3 and sell-3 signals.

→ Robo 4: Most successful robo advisor. It generates buy-4 and sell-4 signals.

→ Super Robo: It combines Robo 1 + Robo 2 + High Volume. It generates super-buy and super-sell signals.

→ Bull & Bear: It is also called a Money Flow. It shows where money goes. To Bulls or Bears.

→ Moon and Hell: It is one of the most chosen robo-advisors for all types of traders.

→ EngineeringRobo's cloud: Inspired by Ichimoku cloud and uses a unique formula. It generates the cloud-buy and cloud-sell signals.

→ Ultimate Moving Average Crossover (UMAC): The most successful moving average crossover signal ever. It generates the golden cross and death cross signals.

→ Early Bird 🦉 : High Risk & High Reward signals.

Engineeringrobo (2 + 3) is not a robo-advisor. It only shows signals if Robo 2 and Robo 3 signals cover each other. So, it is good to keep this function open when you use Robo 2 and Robo 3 at the same time.

HOW TO PICK WINNING CRYPTOCURRENCIES

Since 2017, I have trained and mentored over 120 people to do the same thing, and many of these people have gone on to duplicate, or in some cases exceed, my success. In the following notes, I will share the system I have relied upon and perfected with you.

With several thousand cryptos to choose from, it might seem that finding the right crypto is like looking for a needle in a very large haystack. Fortunately, that isn't the case. Only a tiny percentage of cryptos meet the stringent criteria to make them tradable, given what we're trying to accomplish in a single day-trading session.

Remember, as a swing trader, you're not interested in a particular crypto for holding the lifetime. You're not trying to build a massive, steady portfolio that we can pass on to future generations.

Specifically, you are trying to make $300 on your trades each day. While that might not seem like much, it's more than most people make in an eight-hour day. Over the course of one year, that's an additional $75,000 for just a few extra hours of work each day that's not bad, and you don't have to drive anywhere or dress up for anyone to earn it!

First, you should pick the best three robo-advisors to fit your trading strategy.

Second, you should wait until two robo-advisors give buy signals to you. Then you can buy it with 50% of your stake (Assume that you have $1,000 to invest into the specific coin, you can invest $500 when EngineeringRobo turns bullish).

You should NOT sell more than 50% of your position until 2 robo advisors give you sell signals (It means until EngineeringRobo turns bearish).

☞ 20% of your stake should be invested at the support levels.

☞ Buy with the rest of 30% of your stake when the 1D candle opens & closes above the downtrend line.

Pick the best 3 robo advisors for yourself in your charting platform. If 2 of them are bullish (buy), it is time to buy. Vice versa.

Example: Robo 4 + Robo 2 + Moon & Hell

◯ Buy-4 and Buy-2 signals mean BUY

◯ Sell-4 and Sell-2 signals mean SELL

◯ Buy-4 and Moon signals mean BUY

◯ Sell-4 and Hell signals mean SELL

There is also nothing wrong with selling 50% of your position when you doubled your money to take your initial investment back- Play with a free money strategy.

Keep in mind that you should never sell your position either at the resistance levels or after you get 2 sell signals. Go for a 50/50 strategy. With this, you are less likely to pull your hair out when your coin goes up after you sell. The goal is to make substantial profits on your cryptos and not be upset if the price continues to advance after you get out.

I have seen so many times where unsuccessful traders constantly change their trading styles. Stick to your strategy with EngineeringRobo until you get the results that you are looking for.

⚠ Remember to turn on your candle color feature on your charts. It is in EngineeringRobo Deluxe.

HOW TO USE ENGINEERINGROBO ON CHARTS

1. We chose 3 robo advisors here which are Robo 4, Hell & Moon, and Super Robo Signals. See the chart below.

2. On Nov 20, 2020, we got 2 buy signals, Buy-4 and Moon. It was enough for us to buy the coin. (2 different buy signals are enough to buy).

3. On Feb 28, 2021, we received the Sell-4 signal. Are we selling it? No! Because it was only 1 sell signal was present. (Need 2 different sell signals to sell)

4. On April 24, 2021 we received 2 sell signals, Hell and Sell-4. It was time to close at least 50% of the position here if not all with **1232% - 13.3x profit** in 5 months!

5. On May 8, 2021, Buy-4 and Moon signals were present, it was time to buy. However, we received 2 sell signals shortly and closed our position with a **20% loss**. After we closed our position, the coin dropped as low as 59.14%. Sell signals saved us from the big drop.

6. On July 28, 2021, we received Buy-4 and Moon signals. It means that 2 different buy signals were present out of 3. So, we bought it without waiting for the super buy signal.

7. On November 16 we closed at least 50% of our position with **75% profit** after receiving Sell-4 and Hell signals.

8. Between Nov 20, 2020, and Nov 21, 2021, we only made 3 trades here! 1230% profit, 75% Profit, and 20% Loss

9. On Jan 31, 2022, we got a Buy-4 signal and on Feb 4, 2022, we got a Moon signal. After the second buy signal, we bought the coin. April 6, 2022, we closed our position with a break even. After we closed our

position, the coin dropped as low as 53%. Sell signals saved us from the big drop.

10. On July 18, 2022, we bought the coin after getting Buy-4 and Moon signals from EngineeringRobo. August 19, 2022, we closed our position with a 10% loss. After we closed our position, the coin dropped as low as 16%.

11. On Nov 6, 2022, FTX coin dropped 94.19% after EngineeringRobo gave two sell signals.

● Your $1000 investment has turned into **$382** since Nov 20, 2020, with a buy-and-hold strategy.

● Your $1000 investment has turned into **$18,620.0** since Nov 18, 2020, with EngineeringRobo signals.

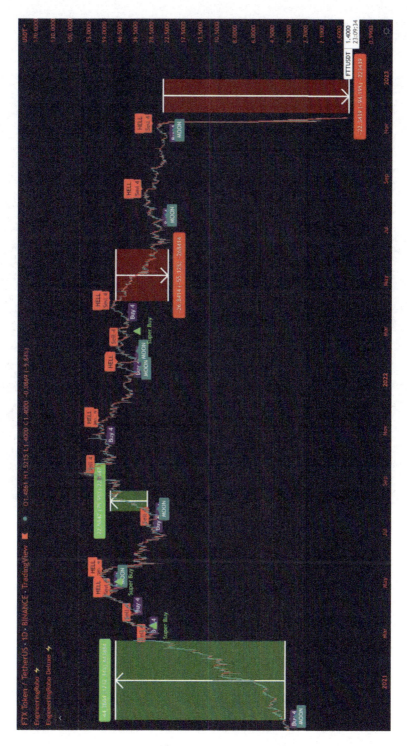

ALGORITHMIC TRADING IN CRYPTO | 91

BULL MARKET CASE STUDIES

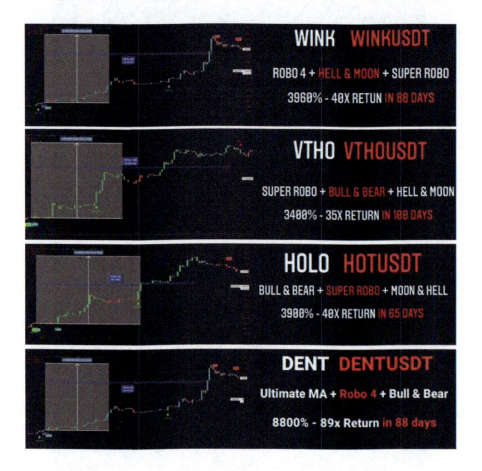

BEAR MARKET CASE STUDIES

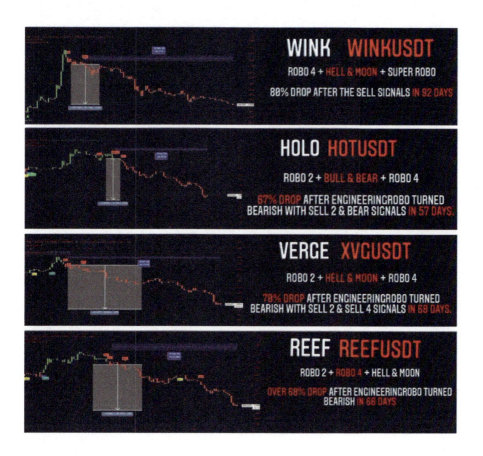

ENGINEERINGROBO'S CRYPTO PORTFOLIO MANAGEMENT TOOL

Professional traders rarely have just one asset within their portfolio. Therefore, to juggle all their investments and trades, they need specific tools to be efficient while trading. By tracking your portfolio and measuring your performance, you can easily improve upon it and make better trades. As the saying goes, you can't improve what you can't measure.

When it comes to crypto portfolio management, you want to know how much of a particular asset you hold and where it is stored. You also want to know how much you are gaining or losing from a particular trade or investment.

Follow the portfolio management strategy below. Swing traders must be familiar with this portfolio management tool to maximize returns.

1) EngineeringRobo gives BUY-4 and MOON signals to Bitcoin on a 1D chart, keep the ratio below on your portfolio:

⬤ 30- 50% ALTCOINS ⬤ 30- 50% BTC ⬤ 10- 20% USDT

2) EngineeringRobo gives BUY 4 and MOON signals to Bitcoin on a 1D chart and you also see any of the conditions below

- Buy 1 - Buy 2 - Buy 3 - Bull - Golden Cross - EngineeringRobo's Green cloud buy - Super Buy

Your portfolio should be ⬤ 40- 50% ALTCOINS ⬤ 30- 50% BTC ⬤ 10% USDT

3) EngineeringRobo gives either SELL-4 or HELL to Bitcoin on a 1D chart, keep the ratio below on your portfolio:

◯ 20- 30% USDT ◯ 30- 40% BTC ◯ 30- 40% ALTCOINS

*Could take profit from all open trades.

4) EngineeringRobo gives both SELL-4 and HELL signals to Bitcoin on a 1D chart, keep the ratio below on your portfolio:

◯ 40- 50% USDT ◯ 30% BTC ◯ 20- 30% ALTCOINS

5) EngineeringRobo gives SELL-4 and HELL signals to Bitcoin on a 1D chart and you also see any of the conditions below

- Sell 1 - Sell 2 - Sell 3 - Bear - Death Cross - EngineeringRobo's Red cloud sell - Super Sell

Your portfolio should be ◯ 50- 70% USDT ◯ 20- 30% BTC ◯ 10- 30% ALTCOINS

DEVELOP YOUR OWN STRATEGY IN ENGINEERINGROBO

You must still find your own place in the market. I may be a 45-minute, and you may be a 3-hour trader. Some may be daily (swing traders) or weekly traders. There's a place in the crypto market for everyone. Consider what you are learning in this book as pieces of a puzzle that together make up the bigger picture of trading. You're going to acquire some pieces here, you're going to pick up pieces on your own from your own reading and research, and eventually, you will create a puzzle that will develop into your own unique trading strategy.

The key, for now, is that you master one strategy. Once you can tread water in the market with your one strategy, you can be a trader without blowing up your account. This is simply a matter of spending time in the chair. The more time you spend watching your charts, the more you will learn. This is a job where you survive until you can make it. You can start casting out later, but first, you need to master just one strategy. It can be the support and resistance strategy, it can be a technical chart pattern strategy, it can be an EngineeringRobo strategy, or you can create a strategy of your own.

Narrow the choices down, develop that area of strength into a workable strategy, and then use that strategy to survive until you are able to develop others. It is absolutely critical for every trader to be trading a strategy. Plan a trade and trade the plan. I wish someone had said this to me when I first started trading. If you're trading with real money, you must be trading a written strategy, and it must have historical data to verify that it's worth trading with real money." You cannot change your plan when you have already entered the trade and have an open position.

The truth about traders is that they fail. They lose money, and a large percentage of those traders are not getting the education that you are receiving from this book. They're going to be using live trading strategies that are not even hammered out, they will just be haphazardly trading a little of this and a little of that until their account is gone, and then they will wonder what happened. You don't want to live trade a new strategy until you've proven that it's worth investing in. You may practice for three months with small size money. There is no shame in reducing your size for new strategies at any stage of your trading career. Even experienced and professional traders, when they want to develop a new strategy, test it out with small-size portfolio.

Remember, the market is always going to be there. You don't need to rush this. A trading career is a marathon and not a sprint. It's not about making $50,000 by the end of next week. It's about developing a set of skills that will last a lifetime.

Continue your education and reflect upon your trading strategy. Never stop learning about the crypto market and crypto cycles. It's a dynamic environment and it's constantly changing. Trading is different than it was ten years ago, and it will be different in another ten years. So, keep reading and discussing your progress and performance with mentors and other professional traders. Always think ahead and maintain a progressive attitude. Learn as much as you can, but keep a degree of healthy skepticism about everything, including this book. Ask questions and do not follow experts solely by their word.

Last but not least, join a community of traders. Trading alone is very difficult and can be emotionally overwhelming. It is very helpful to join a community of traders so you can ask them questions, talk to them, learn new methods and strategies, get some hints and alerts about the stock market, and also make your own contributions. That's why we created the EngineeringRobo chat group. I don't expect everything I do to work exactly the same for you. That's why I am happy to help you develop a strategy that is going to work for you, your personality, your account size, and your risk tolerance when you reach out to us.

PART VI

BITCOIN RALLIES MOST LIKELY START IN OCTOBER. SO, WHAT IS NEXT? 100
FOCUS ON WHAT YOU CAN CONTROL AS A TRADER 102
THE ART OF EXIT LEVELS - CRYPTO PUMP & DUMP 108
IS FUNDAMENTAL NEWS FUNDAMENTALLY USELESS IN BULL MARKETS? 111
IS FUNDAMENTAL NEWS FUNDAMENTALLY USELESS IN BEAR MARKETS? 113
CRYPTOCURRENCY TAX GUIDE 115
TOP FINANCE MOVIES EVERY TRADER SHOULD WATCH 116
BEST TRADING AND INVESTING BOOKS TO READ 118

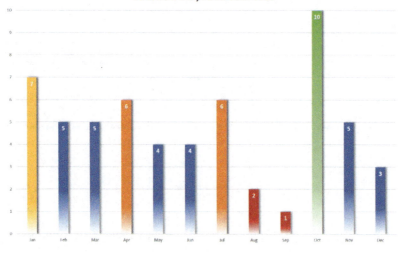

BITCOIN RALLIES MOST LIKELY START IN OCTOBER. SO, WHAT IS NEXT?

October has an 83% probability of starting a new Bitcoin rally. Out of 12 years a rally started in 10 years. Is this information enough to make a huge profit in crypto market?

No! You need a strong trading system and follow the recommendations below to maximize your profit. EngineeringRobo provides a clear framework for trades, which helps reduce uncertainty and confusion. It could be seen as a digital mentor that holds your hand and helps to avoid overtrading. It also includes executing its buy and sell signals in a disciplined manner.

1. Don't get out of a trade because you are afraid to give back some profits!

Instead wait patiently for two different sell signals even if your profits go down again. EngineeringRobo needs some leeway to stay in during minor pullback in order to make potentially more gains in future. If you do not give EngineeringRobo this freedom, you may get out early in a bull run and miss out on future gains. If you cannot resist the urge to take profits, it would be better to exit only 50% of your position depending on technical analysis and let the rest ride until sell signals occur.

2. Don't ignore sell signals because you think the market is destined to go higher!

EngineeringRobo always give sell signals in a timely manner if it detects high probabilities of a down trend. If the trend should nevertheless not change, it should tell you to get in again. This might involve missing some gains, but you also avoid the risk getting caught in a quickly descending price spiral.

3. Don't change your robo advisors continuously!

Especially if you are in a trade. This could turn a profitable trade using the old rules into a loss trade with the new rules. If you found another promising strategy, wait for the next trade. Switching trading rules or robo advisors too often increases your risk of locking in losses.

4. Don't change your position size based on one or two previous loss or win trades!

Don't double your position size because you made a huge gain with a previous trade. If your next trade is a losing one, you might give back more profits than necessary. Also, don't reduce your position size by a large percentage because losing trades. You may lock in your losses because a smaller position size does not allow you to make back lost money. It is better to increase or decrease the position size slowly.

FOCUS ON WHAT YOU CAN CONTROL AS A TRADER

1. Risk Per Trade:

You should never keep more than 10% of your total portfolio in any altcoins in the spot market.

You should never invest more than 1% of your total portfolio amount into any altcoins in the futures market.

2. Entry:

Our entry levels are

→ When EngineeringRobo turns bullish with two different buy signals.

→ When the daily candle touches the support line & uptrend line.

→ When the daily candle is re-testing the triangle after a break-up.

→ When the resistance lines turn into support lines.

→ When the daily candle opens/closes above the downtrend line.

→ When the daily candle breaks open/close its previous all-time high (ATH) level.

3. Exit

Our exit levels are

→ When EngineeringRobo turns bearish with two different sell signals.

→ When we double our investment- 100% gain.

→ When the daily candle is re-testing the triangle after break-down.

→ When the support lines turn into resistance lines.

→ When the daily candle opens/closes below the uptrend line.

→ When the daily candle touches the resistance lines.

→ When the daily candle breaks open/close its previous all-time low (ATL) level.

4. Trade Frequency:

It is all depending on EngineeringRobo's signals and crypto market conditions.

	YEAR	2022				
	MONTH	NOVEMBER				
	Monday	Tuesday	Wednesday	Thursday	Friday	Weekly P/L
Date	1	2	3	4	5	
P/L	-$36	$77	-$160	$147	$34	$62
Commissions/Fees	$28	$14	$65	$46	$27	$180
Total after Comm.	-$64	$63	-$225	$101	$7	-$118 (16 trades)
Date	8	9	10	11	12	
P/L	-$233	$135	$148	$205	-$59	$196
Commissions/Fees	$45	$17	$17	$22	$19	$120
Total after Comm.	-$278	$118	$131	$183	-$78	$76 (12 trades)
Date	15	16	17	18	19	
P/L	$28	$126	$123	$83	$47	$407
Commissions/Fees	$11	$34	$33	$26	$0	$104
Total after Comm.	$17	$92	$90	$57	$47	$303 (11 trades)
Date	22	23	24	25	26	
P/L	$85	$58	$67	Thanksgiving	-$84	$294
Commissions/Fees	$29	$0	$14		$0	$43
Total after Comm.	$56	$58	$53		-$84	$251 (9 trades)
Date	29	30				
P/L	-$26	-$15				-$41
Commissions/Fees	$14	$12				$26
Total after Comm.	-$40	-$27				-$67 (2 trades)
	Total # Trades	50			TOTAL	$918

KEEPING A TRADING JOURNAL – A STRUGGLE ALL TRADERS FACE

Keep track of all your trading activities in a trading journal. Doing so eventually turns your trading journal into a reference manual that can become an invaluable tool for helping you recall what you've done to identify what works and what doesn't. A trading journal also can help you analyze your trades and trading systems to determine which aspects of trading you do well and which ones you need to work on.

When you develop a trading system, save ideas and test results in your journal. When you enter a position, record everything about the trade. Include your thoughts as you contemplate making the trade. When you have a what-was-I-thinking moment, later on, you can find the answer in your journal.

At a minimum, your notes need to include the following:

→ Trade date
→ Crypto ticker

- Three robo-advisors you chose
- Whether you bought long or sold short
- Which strategy triggered the entry signal (Like Support and resistance strategy, EngineeringRobo strategy)
- Which strategy triggered the exit signal (Like Chart pattern strategy, Pre-set stop loss)
- Which time frame you chose
- What caused you to exit the position
- The percentage gain or loss from the trade
- Your thoughts, hopes, and fears that you had before opening the position and while the position was open

You can improve only the things that you measure. Record statistics about your trades. Include the duration of each trade. After you close a trade, write down what you might have done differently. Find out whether you can identify signals that can help you recognize similar situations in future trades.

Although keeping the journal is important, it is useful only when you review it regularly. Spend a little time every week or month reviewing all your trades, so you can pinpoint consistent mistakes or missed opportunities. Many traders discover more from their failures than from their successes. Try figuring out why your failed trades didn't work and what you could've done to improve your results.

Of course, don't ignore your successes. After all, you need to know what works and why and then try to incorporate those winning strategies more consistently into your trading system.

TOP 3 CRYPTO TRADING SELL STRATEGIES

Cryptocurrency sell strategies are an important consideration for traders in the digital asset market. With the volatility and uncertainty that characterizes the crypto market, having a well-defined plan for selling a position can help investors manage risk and maximize returns. Traders have many different sell strategies they can use.

Depending on market cycles, certain strategies will perform better than others. Ideally, a sell strategy will allow traders to make more money than their initial investment, but it should also protect them from large losses if the market moves against them. Below are the 4 best cryptocurrency sell strategies traders can use in order to make significant gains and protect their losses in the long term.

1. Sell at specific price targets

Price targets involve meeting a specific price point before selling your investment. This strategy can be used to take profits at regular intervals or to cash out completely after the price reaches a certain level. The benefits of using price targets include disciplined selling and the ability to take advantage of short-term price movements.

For example, a trader who buys Bitcoin at $14,000 might set a target price of $20,000 and sell half of their holdings when it reaches that level.

It is important to remember that market volatility and large price swings are common features of the cryptocurrency markets. Therefore, it may take a long time to reach your target price or it may be reached quickly and then exceeded. Because of this, it is essential to have patience when applying this strategy and to be prepared to adjust your price target if crypto market conditions change.

2. Sell by portfolio

The portfolio sell strategy involves selling all of your crypto investments in a particular crypto or group of cryptocurrencies once they reach a certain level of return.

The benefits of this strategy include simplifying your investment portfolio and taking profits regularly. The downside of this strategy, however, is that you may miss out on potential gains if the crypto you sell increases in value. Therefore, price targets might be a better choice for you if FOMO is an issue for you when trading.

To sell by portfolio, you will need to set a target return for each of your investments. Once an investment reaches your target return, you can sell your holdings and reinvest the proceeds into another cryptocurrency.

3. Sell by specific return (%)

Crypto traders can also sell by their return percentage. This strategy is similar to the portfolio sell strategy, but with one key difference. The main idea behind this strategy is to sell your investment once it has reached a certain percentage return, regardless of current market value.

For example, if you buy Ethereum for $1,000 and it increases in value to $1,500, you would have made a 50% return on your investment. If you had set a target return of 40%, you would sell your investment and take your profits once it hit 40% ($1,400) meaning a guaranteed return but the potential to miss out if the market value continues to increase to $1,500.

Bonus: Sell by EngineeringRobo

The crypto market is highly volatile, which can make it difficult to know when to sell your assets. This strategy involves selling your cryptocurrencies depending on EngineeringRobo signals. First, you must pick three different robo advisors, you will need to stick to it in order to take advantage of the strategy. Once you get two different sell signals, you can place an order to sell your holdings.

THE ART OF EXIT LEVELS - CRYPTO PUMP & DUMP

The strategy is so simple: buy low-volume crypto, pump up its potential returns to investors on Twitter, Telegram, Discord, and other social networks, promise huge returns, and then dump the position when the buying starts and the price spikes.

The time between getting in at the bottom and holding the bag at the end can be less than one hour. It's rarely more than a week.

☞ The easiest way to spot a pump and dump is to start by understanding its mechanics. If the value of a relatively unknown coin rises suddenly without reason, there's a good chance manipulation is at play.

☞ It's always best to do some digging before making a purchase.

Review the chart carefully to understand it well.

It is always great to take profit at the resistance levels, when you double your money or when EngineeringRobo turns bearish.

You bought at the support level; however, the daily candle broke down the support level. So, what should you do?

You can always sell when the candle opens / closes below the support level with a loss.

If you missed selling your coin at the right time, some of the coins might re-visit the support & resistance levels again after it broke them. At that time, you should sell your position if you bought at the support level.

⚠️ If you are following any EngineeringRobo signals, you should always wait for the candle close before buying or selling. I also do not recommend our members to chase the pump.

🎯 **Pro-tip:** Support and resistance levels are extremely important concepts in technical trading. Being able to accurately determine these two levels is important to improve the profitability of trades and your short-term trading strategy. For this reason, traders and investors should use support and resistance levels with EngineeringRobo signals to get the best results.

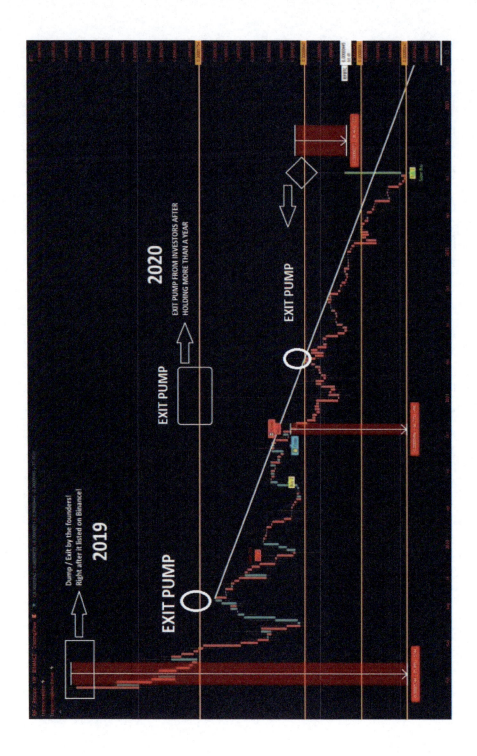

IS FUNDAMENTAL NEWS FUNDAMENTALLY USELESS IN BULL MARKETS?

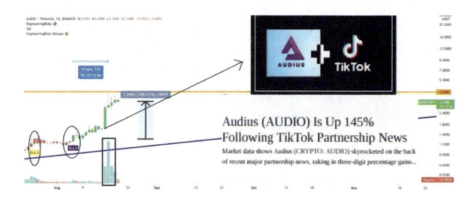

Let's look at the chart of AUDIOUSDT chart. After the partnership news, Audio went up over 145%!

The best thing was EngineeringRobo already gave you buy signals a week earlier! How?

👉 Followed the market makers and insider activity on candles!

I am not saying that you should totally ignore fundamental news (partnership, upgrade, fork, or events), however, your decision in crypto should be based on:

→ 50% EngineeringRobo

→ 30% Technical Analysis

→ 20% Experience + Fundamental analysis

Let's look at the FILUSDT chart. Was Grayscale, one of the biggest crypto funds, accumulating FILECOIN for months before sharing this news on media?

Maybe! They knew that people would increase the price of the coin after the news. It is normal for them to share this news on media when they were done with accumulating.

Big crypto funds have had it their own way for a very, very long time. They get information before the rest of us... and they use it. We can't stop that. But we can level the playing field!

EngineeringRobo's buy signals came in the first week of January 2021 when FILECOIN was around $20.

The price was already $80 when the fundamental news was available to the public.

◎ **Pro-tip:** So, don't get distracted by fundamental analysis when you trade crypto or futures. Fundamentals are key for long-term investors, but traders will likely find that their analysis doesn't improve their performance on short-term trades.

IS FUNDAMENTAL NEWS FUNDAMENTALLY USELESS IN BEAR MARKETS?

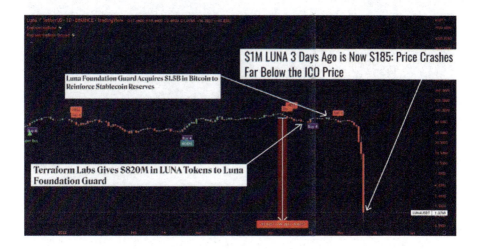

The Terra (LUNA) crypto token first crashed from $120 to $0.02, a 99.9% correction, of which 99% was within 48 hours of a black swan event on May 11 – 12, 2022.

The LUNA crash continued a further 99%, then again, and finally another 90% drop to reach $0.00000112 against BUSD (Binance USD), the last trading pair to not be delisted by crypto exchanges. So how did it happen?

On 9 May, after nearly 18 months of steadily holding its value against the US dollar, the so-called stable coin TerraUSD (UST) became unpegged, and LUNA started to drop. We can talk about this for days, but I actually want to show you EngineeringRobo signals here.

EngineeringRobo gave two different sell signals on April 10, 2022 while everyone else was still bullish. At that time, LUNA was around $94. After EngineeringRobo turned bearish with two sell signals, LUNA dropped almost $0.

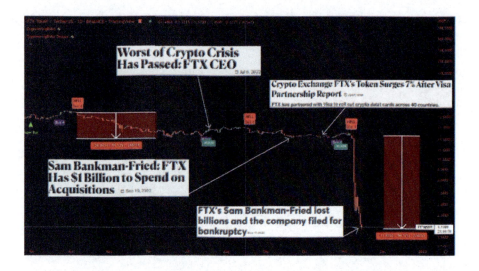

Months after Terra, Three Arrows Capital, and a host of other industry-leading firms imploded, the crypto space has been hit by another major wipeout. At its peak, FTX was valued at $32 billion. The company filed for bankruptcy on Nov. 11, 2022. So how did it happen?

FTX had $16B in customer assets, it lent billions of dollars in user funds to its sister company Alameda Research to fund risky bets. We can talk about this for days, but I actually want to show you EngineeringRobo signals here. FTX's main token is FTT which is a utility token utilized to reduce the trading fees and for several more utilities on the platform.

EngineeringRobo gave two different sell signals to FTT on Nov 6, 2022 while everyone else was still bullish. At that time, FTT was around $22. After EngineeringRobo turned bearish with two sell signals, FTT dropped around $1.

The lessons this industry will have to (re)learn to unearth itself from this crisis, however, will be the same ones it has always preached. Rule 1: Follow EngineeringRobo signals in both and bear markets; and Rule 2: Never forget rule 1.

CRYPTOCURRENCY TAX GUIDE

In this guide, you will learn everything you need to know about Bitcoin and cryptocurrency taxation in North America. If you've bought and sold cryptocurrency in the last calendar year, it's time to start thinking about the impact this may have on your income tax return. Whether you've made a profit or a loss trading cryptocurrency, you'll need to declare it in your annual tax return.

In North America, cryptocurrency is generally treated as a commodity, which means it is taxed as either income or capital gain. It's essential that you understand the tax consequences of your specific situation when it comes to buying, selling, and trading crypto. In this book, we look at the basics of cryptocurrency tax in Canada to help you learn what you need to do to keep the taxman happy.

Before we dig into the weeds of capital gains in Canada, there's something you should know. This is general information on capital gains to give you a better understanding of how it works. Since everyone's situation is unique, this should not be taken as advice and you should always consult a tax professional to determine what works best in your specific situation.

How is cryptocurrency taxed?

The profit made from cryptocurrency is determined in Canadian dollars when you exchange cryptocurrency for fiat or cryptocurrency, or you use it for goods and services.

For example, if you buy or otherwise obtain 1 BTC when it's worth $10,000, and then sell or spend it all when it's worth $18,000, you've made a capital gain of $8,000. Capital gains have a tax obligation of 50%, meaning you'd have to pay tax on 50% of the gain.

TOP FINANCE MOVIES EVERY TRADER SHOULD WATCH

1. Wall Street — A young and impatient stockbroker is willing to do anything to get to the top, including trading on illegal inside information taken through a ruthless and greedy corporate raider who takes the youth under his wing.

2. Wolf of Wall Street — Based on the true story of Jordan Belfort, from his rise to a wealthy stock-broker living the high life to his fall involving crime, corruption and the federal government.

3. The Big Short — In 2006-2007 a group of investors bet against the US mortgage market. In their research, they discover how flawed and corrupt the market is.

4. Margin Call — This is how it might have looked inside Lehman Brothers the days and hours before it went bankrupt.

5. Trading Places — A snobbish investor and a wily street con artist find their positions reversed as part of a bet by two callous millionaires. You will never look at orange juice futures the same again.

6. Too Big To Fail — Based on Andrew Ross Sorkin's non-fiction book. Learn what happened during the 2008/09 Financial Crisis.

7. Boiler Room — A college dropout, attempting to live up to his father's high standards, gets a job as a broker for a suburban investment firm which puts him on the fast track to success. But the job might not be as legitimate as it first appeared to be.

8. Inside Job — A fantastic in-depth and unique dive into what sparked the Financial Crisis.

9. Enron: The Smartest Guys In The Room —A documentary about the Enron corporation, its faulty and corrupt business practices, and how they led to its fall. The story behind one of biggest frauds in corporate history.

10. Rogue Trader —The story of Nick Leeson, an ambitious investment broker who singlehandedly bankrupted one of the oldest and most important banks in Britain with a few hidden and terrible trades.

11. American Psycho — A wealthy New York City investment banking executive, Patrick Bateman, hides his alternate psychopathic ego from his co-workers and friends as he delves deeper into his violent, hedonistic fantasies.

12. Other People's Money — One of the lesser-known investing movies out there. Danny Devito plays a corporate raider however and it's pretty entertaining.

13. Arbitrage — A hedge fund manager is about to get really rich. But it's built on lies and one really big crime.

14. Moneyball— The movie tells the true story of an underfunded baseball team that also focused on "stealing bases" instead of trying to hit home runs. "Here's the key to trading success: small profits, consistently."

> "Remember there are no short cuts son, quick buck artists come and go with every bull market but the steady players make it through the bear markets." - Wall Street (1987)

BEST TRADING AND INVESTING BOOKS TO READ

1. Market Wizards: Interviews with Top Traders — Market Wizards is one of the most fascinating books ever written about Wall Street. Features interviews with superstar money-makers including Bruce Kovner, Richard Dennis, Paul Tudor Jones, Michel Steinhardt, Ed Seykota, Marty Schwartz, Tom Baldwin, and more.

2. How I made $2,000,000 in the stock market — Excellent book for those starting out with investing. It provides a good foundation to build. Even though the book was written a long time ago there are many principles still in effect.

3. How to Make Money in Stocks: A Winning System in Good Times and Bad — The book is highly informative with plain and simple common-sense investing which is fully backed up with long-term research.

4. How To Trade In Stocks — Jessie Livermore was a god-father trader – the book is packed full of time-tested trading strategy.

5. The Disciplined Trader: Developing Winning Attitudes — The Disciplined Trader helps you join the elite few who have learned how to control their trading behavior.

6. The Intelligent Investor — By far one of the best books on investing ever written.

7. Reminiscences of a Stock Operator — A must-read classic for all investors, whether brand-new or experienced.

8. The Millionaire Next Door: The Surprising Secrets of America's Wealthy — Even though the research is based on America's wealth, it's interesting to see how the habits of the wealthy can be replicated wherever you are in the world.

9. One up on Wall Street: How to Use What You Already Know to Make Money in the Market — The manager of a top investment fund discusses how individuals can make a killing in the market through research and investment techniques that confound conventional market wisdom.

10. Learn to Earn: A Beginner's Guide to the Basics of Investing and Business — For those who know what to look for, investment opportunities are everywhere.

11. Principles for Dealing with the Changing World Order: Why Nations Succeed or Fail — If you love economics with a mix of history, this is a must-have book.

12. Think and Grow Rich — "Think and Grow Rich" is a motivational personal development and self-help book written by Napoleon Hill.

13. Trading In The Zone — The book provides helpful resources and tools to improve your psychology and how to handle winning and losing.

◎ **Pro-tip:** Financial trading is a massive business and there are thousands of books on the subject. Not every book is a must-read and there are lots that provide little or no useful information. However, a great trading book can take your trading to the next level.

PART VII

HOW TO INVEST $1 MILLION IN TODAY'S MARKET — 122

HOW I HAVE LOST AROUND $88,000 IN FUTURES MARKET SINCE 2016? — 125

HOW ISAAC NEWTON LOST $4 MILLION IN THE SOUTH SEA BUBBLE OF 1720? — 127

STRESS MANAGEMENT IN THE TRADING DAY — 129

CRYPTO MARKET CYCLES — 132

HOW TO INVEST $1 MILLION IN TODAY'S MARKET

I once had an EngineeringRobo member ask me, "if you had a million dollars, how would you invest it?". If you have a million dollars to invest or anywhere close to that, the steps below can help you grow your money so it lasts a lifetime for someone between 30 and 45 years old.

1. 10% - $100,000 in commodities

5% - $50,000 in Silver - 5% - $50,000 in Gold

2. 5% - $50,000 in cash

Keep this money for a rainy day. Don't touch it until it is your last chance.

3. 5% - $50,000 in Checking & Saving Accounts

To cover your daily spending. Vacation & Unexpected expenses.

4. 15% - $150,000 in valuable assets

9% - $90,000 in a car - 6% - $60,000 in used Rolex, jewelry, collectibles or other valuable things

5. 20% - $200,000 in Real Estate

You can use this money for the down payment of your real estate purchase.

☞ Primary Residence ☞ Commercial Real Estate ☞ REIT ☞ Land

6. 20% - $200,000 in stock market

10% - $100,000 ☞ VOO ☞ TSE: VFV ☞ VTI

10% - $50,000 in individual stocks like PYPL, FB, SQ, SPCE, BYND, ZM, HOOD, BABA, WEED, etc...

7. 25% - $250,000 in Cryptocurrencies

☞ 15% - $150,000 in 3 different crypto exchanges.

$50,000 in Bitcoin - $75,000 in Altcoins - $25,000 in USDT

☞ 8% - $80,000 in Investment account on Ledger & Trezor.

☞ 2% - $20,000 in NFTs.

▶ You can invest in NFT projects or virtual lands on NFT marketplaces like OpenSea, Rarible, or Orderinbox.

The ROAD TO FINANCIAL FREEDOM WITH ENGINEERINGROBO

Balanced Portfolio % for 18 - 35 years old

USED FOR: Between 18 and 35	
INVESTMENT	MARKET SHARE
Cryptocurrencies	40%
Stocks	20%
Side Hustle Business	15%
Valuable Assets (Car, ...)	10%
Cash	10%
Precious Metals (Gold, Silver, etc.)	5%

Balanced Portfolio % for 35 - 45 years old

USED FOR: Between 35 and 45	
INVESTMENT	MARKET SHARE
Cryptocurrencies	20%
Real Estate	20%
Stock	20%
Valuable Assets (Car, Paintings, etc.)	15%
Business	15%
Cash	5%
Precious Metals (Gold, Silver, etc.)	5%

Balanced Portfolio % for 45 - 55 years old

USED FOR: Between 45 and 55	
INVESTMENT	MARKET SHARE
Mutual Funds + Bonds + Stocks	35%
Business	25%
Primary Residence + Real Estate	20%
Valuable Assets (Car, Paintings, etc.)	5%
Cryptocurrencies	5%
Cash	5%
Precious Metals (Gold, Silver, etc.)	5%

Balanced Portfolio % for 55 and older

USED FOR: 55 and older	
INVESTMENT	MARKET SHARE
Mutual Funds + Bonds + Stocks	30%
Primary Residence + Real Estate	30%
Business	10%
Retirement (Pension) + Managed Asset	10%
Cash	10%
Gold, Silver, Cryptocurrencies	5%
Valuable Assets (Car, Paintings, etc.	5%

HOW I HAVE LOST AROUND $88,000 IN FUTURES MARKET SINCE 2016?

Between 2016 and 2021, I've been liquidated 5 times in my futures portfolio and lost around $88,000. How did it happen? Let me explain step by step here.

1. **Black Swan Events** - Every 6-month crypto market pumps or dumps over 30% unexpectedly. At one time I had many long positions, the market flash crashed, and my position was instantly liquidated!

2. **Averaging down positions** - I was averaging down a coin on leverage in 2018. Hoping to recover one day. The coin lost almost 99% of its value. My profits and elation were short-lived, however, as one of the crypto prices soon rebounded to new lows and then moved unrelentingly lower: 42 cents, 18 cents, 9 cents, and 2 cents. Finally, with my account equity wiped out, I was forced to liquidate the position.

3. **High Leverage** - At the beginning of my futures market journey, I was testing between 50X - 100X. It was going so well in the first month. I tripled my money. Then the market plummeted like a stone. I lost all my trading capital.

4. **All in** - I was using all my futures stake per trade. I opened a short position but the coin started to go up. I felt that I should get out, but I just watched. I was totally paralyzed. I was hoping the market would turn around. I watched and watched and then after it locked limit-down, I couldn't get out. I received a margin call and my position was liquidated at market price.

5. **Too many trades** - I was trading over 10 times per day. I burned out. At one point, the market liquidated me. After that scary experience, I never really overtraded again.

One of my worst years was 2018. The bull markets had ended, but I kept trying to hold on and buy back in at lower prices. The markets just kept on breaking. I had never seen a major bear market before, so I was all set up for an important educational experience. Bear markets have different characteristics than bull markets.

As you can see, I've probably made all the possible trading mistakes in the futures market since 2016, and I lost so much money.

Losing money is a good thing. When you know why you lost money, you are not going to do it again.

Making money could be a bad thing—if you do not know why you made money, how are you going to do the same things again? The only way you are going to know is by journaling and writing down your trades, with all their details.

One or two bad black swan days could wipe out all your profits accumulated over three to four months of good trading. Furthermore, your losses can keep you from making money in the future. The less capital you have to work with, the less you will have available for trading. Therefore, one of the keys to success is to preserve your capital base—you do this by minimizing your losses.

Look at professional baseball players: The best of the best in their profession only bat .300, which means that they fail to get a hit seven out of every ten times they come to the plate. They fail more than twice as often as they succeed—and those are the great ones. Compared to that level of failure, being an active trader is not that difficult, but if you cannot maintain emotional control and make sound decisions, your active trading days will be short-lived. The highest batting average in Major League Baseball (MLB) history is .366 over 24 seasons from Ty Cobb.

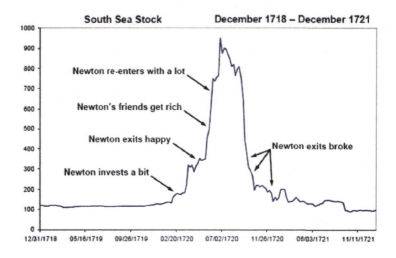

HOW ISAAC NEWTON LOST $4 MILLION IN THE SOUTH SEA BUBBLE OF 1720?

When you think of Sir Isaac Newton (1642 – 1727), what comes to mind? For me, it's an image of him sitting under an apple tree, being hit on the head by falling fruit and suddenly coming up with the law of gravity.

He was one of the most brilliant minds the human race has ever seen. The English physicist and mathematician is legendary in his contributions to the advancement of mankind. Less well known were his speculations on the London Stock Exchange. His investments were usually prudent and profitable. But then, late in life, he placed nearly all of his wealth into the stock of one company.

In the early 1710s, Sir Isaac acquired stocks in the South Sea Company shortly after its launch in 1711. Over the next eight years, he bought stock at about £100 a share, until by the end of 1719 he had accumulated holdings worth £13,000, or roughly £2 million in present-day British currency.

In 1720, the company bagged a deal to manage British government debt. The British government had a large backlog of unpaid bills, largely from contractors supplying the British military during the War of the Spanish Succession. The government offered its creditors South Sea stock, a product similar to shares in a modern corporation. As soon as the news spread, the price of the South Sea stock started soaring. It was the first "bubble" in stock-market history.

By mid-1721, he owned 16,300 stocks. Around April 1720, as the chart above shows, he liquidated most of his South Sea holdings, for a profit of £20,000—or 200 years of his former annual salary as a professor at the University of Cambridge. Newton exited the stock happily. The real problem started here. Even though, Newton has sold off his position in the South Sea. His friends continued to hold it and they made more profit than him. The stock kept soaring. With England in a euphoric mood, watching from the sidelines was hard to do: Newton jumped back in during June and went all in at about £700 a share. Shortly after, the price hit almost £1,000, making the company worth twice the value of all the land in England.

Shortly after, the bubble of the South Sea Company Burst and stock price came down drastically. Newton lost as much as 77% during the bubble, or £24,600. That's around $4 million in today's money.

Sir Isaac Newton, when asked about South Sea stock in the spring of 1721, famously declared that he "could calculate the motions of the heavenly stars, but not the madness of people". For the rest of his life, he forbade anyone to speak the words 'South Sea' in his presence.

The South Sea bubble eventually resulted in one of the biggest financial crashes in London at that time. Though the real reasons behind the bubble are complex, it's among the earliest major manipulations of financial markets.

STRESS MANAGEMENT IN THE TRADING DAY

The key to successful trading is controlling your emotions. After all, the crypto doesn't know that you own it, as traders like to say, so it isn't going to perform well just because you want it to. This can be infuriating, especially when you are going through a draw-down of your capital. Those losses look mighty personal.

If you can't figure out a way to manage your reactions to the crypto market, you shouldn't be a trader. Almost all traders talk about their enemies being fear and greed. If you panic, you'll no longer be trading to win, but trading not to lose. That's an important distinction: If your goal is not to lose, you won't take the appropriate risks, and you won't be able to respond quickly to what the market is telling you.

Controlling your emotions is much easier said than done. Human beings are emotional creatures, constantly reacting (and sometimes overreacting) to everything that happens in their lives. Knowing the emotions that affect trading and having some ways to manage them can greatly improve your overall performance.

Successful traders also have a life outside the markets. They close out their positions, shut off their monitors, and go do something else with the rest of the day. There is no need to be reminded that the market is always open.

Exercise

Exercise keeps your body in fighting shape so that you can stand up to market stress and react to trends when you need to. Many times, when you're trading, you have huge rushes of adrenaline that you can't do much about. You have to stay in front of your screen until the trade is over, no matter how much you want to run away screaming. But after the trading day, you can hit the track or pool or treadmill and burn off some of that adrenaline. Figuring out a regular exercise routine can pay off your trading.

Meditation

When you're trading, you may get upset and start thinking about everything else that has ever gone wrong in your life, instead of staying focused on the task at hand. Even after you close out your positions and shut down your monitors, your day's trading may keep playing itself out over and over in your head, making it impossible for you to relax. Crypto trading requires mental discipline.

Friends and family

Trading is a lonely activity. You work by yourself all day. It's just you, your room, and your screen. This job is really isolating. If you don't get other human contacts, you run the risk of personalizing the market in order not to feel so lonely. That's bad because the market isn't a person; it's an agglomeration of all the financial activity taking place, and it has no interest in you whatsoever. If you like pets, consider getting one to keep you company during the day. There's nothing like a pet that keeps you energetic.

Hobbies and other interests

A lot of people get into day trading because they have long had a fascination with the market. Trading goes from being a hobby to being a living. In many ways, that's perfect. Going to work is so much easier when you have a job that you love. So, find a new hobby if you don't have one. Maybe it's a TV show, a sport, or flying a drone, but whatever it is, you need to have something going on outside of your trading.

Mentors

Most millionaire traders didn't become rich on their own. Rather, they found people whose lifestyles they wanted to emulate and followed what those people did. In other words, they found mentors.

Mentors are people who have already been there and have already done that. They've already made mistakes and broken barriers. While their success won't become your success, they can show you what works and what doesn't. On the road to financial success and wealth, you don't have to fail in the same ways that other people have failed. You can find someone to show you how to do things more efficiently and how to make better financial decisions.

CRYPTO MARKET CYCLES

Learning how market cycles operate can be extremely beneficial to your trading, understanding the true influence of fear and greed. 90% of trading is purely psychology. The psychology of trading defines a specified range of emotions that an investor can go through while making an investment decision. Explained below are the 12 stages of investor emotions:

Stage 1. The Upturn – Optimism, Excitement, Thrill, and Euphoria – "Wow, I feel great about this investment."

When you enter the market, you feel optimistic about investing and confident your risk will pay off in the long run. As the market goes up, your emotions become increasingly positive until they peak with a feeling of euphoria when returns are highest.

Stage 2. The Downturn — Anxiety, Denial, Fear, and Desperation – "Temporary setback. I'm a long-term investor."

As the market starts to dip and your investments lose value, uncertainty will make you feel nervous. You may anxiously watch the market until denial takes over and you regain confidence in your long-term investment strategy. When the market doesn't improve you will become increasingly fearful of losses as you are unsure how far the market will fall.

Stage 3. The Bottom — Panic, Capitulation, Despondency, and Depression – "Maybe the markets just aren't for me."

As the bottom of the cycle is continuing, decline and losses lead to panic. Despondency and depression make you lose hope in the market as you wonder how you could have been so wrong. Ironically, it is when you feel most discouraged about your investments that you have the most to gain — the point of maximum financial opportunity. Feelings of depression and desperation may make you rethink your risk tolerance and tempt you to throw in the towel. Avoid the urge to sell when your portfolio is worth the least. Instead, consider buying while prices are at their lowest.

Stage 4. The Upturn — Hope, Relief, and Optimism

When the market begins to recover you will feel hopeful that it will continue to climb. As conditions continue to improve, hope and relief may also be met with skepticism, as you wonder if the growth will last. As the market recovers and returns to a baseline, you will regain optimism once again feeling enthusiastic about your investment opportunities.

As you ride the emotional roller coaster of the crypto market, it is important to remember the inverse relationship between your feelings and investment opportunities at the peak and valley of the market cycle. While everyone experiences the same emotions as they watch the market performance, successful traders avoid the innate emotional tendency to buy high and sell low by using EngineeringRobo signals.

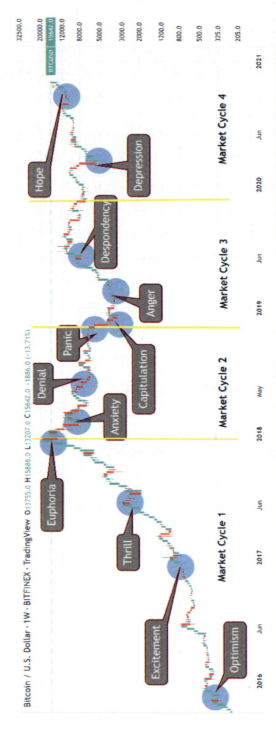

https://www.tradingview.com/chart/BTCUSD/MRDAolbc-The-Roller-Coaster-of-Trader-s-Emotions-12-Steps-are-the-key

PART VIII

THE SUMMARY OF BITCOIN MOVEMENT BETWEEN 2011 AND 2013	136
THE SUMMARY OF BITCOIN MOVEMENT BETWEEN 2013 AND 2016	138
THE SUMMARY OF BITCOIN MOVEMENT BETWEEN 2016 AND 2020	140
THE SUMMARY OF BITCOIN MOVEMENT BETWEEN 2020 AND 2023	142

THE SUMMARY OF BITCOIN MOVEMENT BETWEEN 2011 AND 2013

1. Bitcoin dropped 93% down from an all-time high (ATH).
2. When the weekly candle was below 20-Moving Average (MA) line, Bitcoin dropped 77%.
3. Bitcoin dropped 79% after EngineeringRobo turned bearish with Super Sell, Sell-2, and Hell signals.
4. When the weekly candle was below 50-MA, Bitcoin dropped 58%.
5. 50-MA stayed above 20-MA for 217 days during the bear market. When 50-MA crossed 20-MA, the weekly candle failed to stay above 50-MA after the first attempt, and Bitcoin dropped 46%.

→ The Bull season started after the second attempt.

The weekly candle touched 100-MA, and Bitcoin weekly candle stayed always above 100-MA.

It took 623 days to break ATH again.

● Bull season started when both weekly candles moved over 20-MA and 20-MA crossed above 50-MA.

● Bear season started when BTC was below 20-MA on a weekly chart.

→ When was the best time to buy?

☞ When both weekly candles moved over 20-MA and 20-MA crossed above 50-MA, then it was the right time to open a long position. Bitcoin was at around $6 at that time.

☞ When EngineeringRobo turned bullish with 2 different buy signals (Buy-2 and Moon).

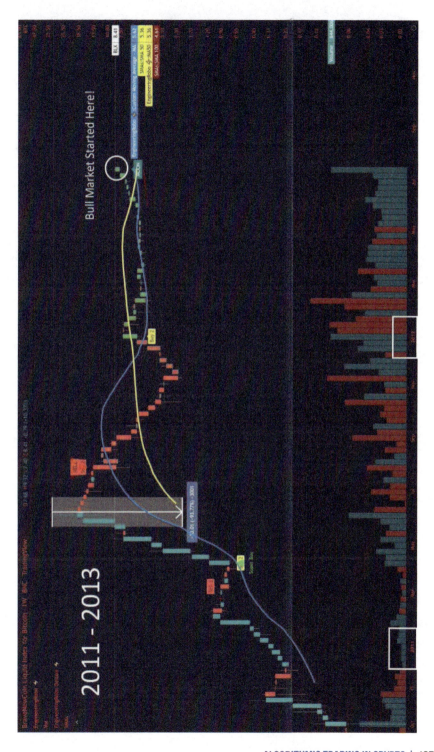

ALGORITHMIC TRADING IN CRYPTO | 137

THE SUMMARY OF BITCOIN MOVEMENT BETWEEN 2013 AND 2016

1. Bitcoin dropped 86% down from an all-time high (ATH).
2. When the weekly candle was below 20-Moving Average (MA) line, Bitcoin dropped 72%.
3. Bitcoin dropped 71% after EngineeringRobo turned bearish with Sell-4 and Hell signals.
4. When the weekly candle was below 50-MA, Bitcoin dropped 68%.
5. 50-MA was above 20-MA for 427 days during the bear market.
When 50-MA crossed 20-MA, the weekly candle failed to stay above 50-MA at the first attempt and Bitcoin dropped 36%. Bitcoin candles were also below 100-MA.

→ The Bull season started after the second attempt.

The weekly candle touched 100-MA, and Bitcoin weekly candle stayed below 100-MA for 357 days.

It took 1134 days to break ATH again.

● Bull season started when both weekly candles moved over 20-MA and 20-MA crossed above 50-MA.

● Bear season started when Bitcoin was below 20-MA on a weekly chart.

→ When was the best time to buy?

☞ When both weekly candles moved over 20-MA and 20-MA crossed above 50-MA, then it was the right time to open a long position. Bitcoin was at around $285 at that time.

☞ When EngineeringRobo turned bullish with 2 different buy signals (Buy-4 and Moon).

ALGORITHMIC TRADING IN CRYPTO | 139

THE SUMMARY OF BITCOIN MOVEMENT BETWEEN 2016 AND 2020

1. Bitcoin dropped 84% down from an all-time high (ATH).
2. When the weekly candle was below 20-Moving Average (MA) line, Bitcoin dropped 60%.
3. Bitcoin dropped 61% after EngineeringRobo turned bearish with Sell-4 and Hell signals.
4. When the weekly candle was below 50-MA, Bitcoin dropped 53%.
5. 50-MA was above 20-MA for 343 days during the bear market. When 50-MA crossed 20-MA, the weekly candle failed to stay above 50-MA at the first attempt and Bitcoin dropped 50%. Bitcoin candles were also below 100-MA.

→ The Bull season started after the second attempt.

The weekly candle touched 100-MA, and Bitcoin weekly candle stayed below 100-MA for 168 days.

It took 1099 days to break ATH again.

● Bull season started when both weekly candles moved over 20-MA and 20-MA crossed above 50-MA.

● Bear season started when Bitcoin was below 20-MA on a weekly chart.

→ When was the best time to buy?

☞ When both weekly candles moved over 20-MA and 20-MA crossed above 50-MA, then it was the right time to open a long position. Bitcoin was at around $7500 at that time.

☞ When EngineeringRobo turned bullish with 2 different buy signals (Buy-4 and Bull)

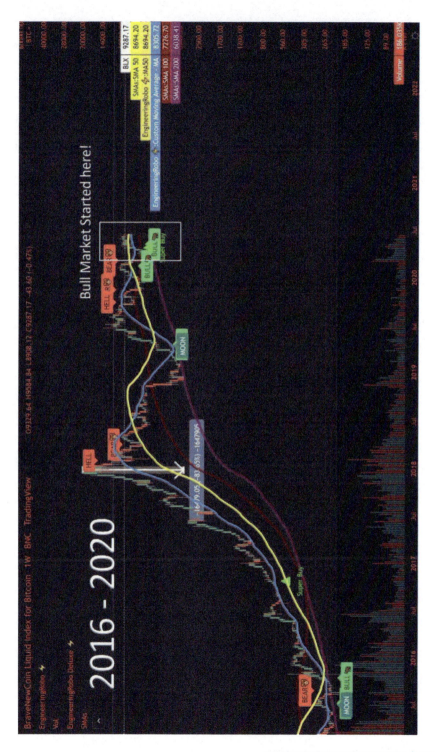

THE SUMMARY OF BITCOIN MOVEMENT BETWEEN 2020 AND 2023

1. Bitcoin dropped 77% down from an all-time high (ATH) so far.
2. When the weekly candle was below 20-Moving Average (MA) line, Bitcoin dropped 68%.
3. Bitcoin dropped 66% after EngineeringRobo turned bearish with Super Sell, Sell-4, and Hell signals.
4. When the weekly candle was below 50-MA, Bitcoin dropped 67%.
5. 50-MA is above 20-MA for 265 days so far.
When 50-MA crossed 20-MA, the weekly candle failed to stay above 50-MA at the first attempt and Bitcoin dropped 58%. Bitcoin candles have been below 100-MA since May 2022.

At the time of writing this book, the weekly candle touched 100-MA, and Bitcoin weekly candle stayed below 100-MA for 224 days.

It might take more than 600 days to break ATH again as of writing. Halving years are officially accepted as the beginning of the bull market in crypto.

⬤ Bull season might start when Bitcoin is above 20-MA on a weekly chart and 20-MA crosses above 50-MA.

⬤ Bear season started when BTC was below 20-MA on a weekly chart.

◎ 1 Bitcoin Average Mining Cost is $17,800 according to https://en.macromicro.me/charts/29435/bitcoin-production-total-cost.

According to J.P. Morgan estimate of Bitcoin's average production cost has dropped from around $20k at the beginning of June to around $15k by the end of June and around $13k at the time of writing.

Historically, BTC dropped an average of 30% below the mining cost during the bear markets.

→ When will be the best time to buy?

☞ When both weekly candles have moved over 20-MA and 20-MA have crossed above 50-MA, then you can open a long position.

☞ When EngineeringRobo turns bullish with 2 different buy signals.

☞ According to our strategy, buying Bitcoin around $14,000 is a very smart decision for long-term investment.

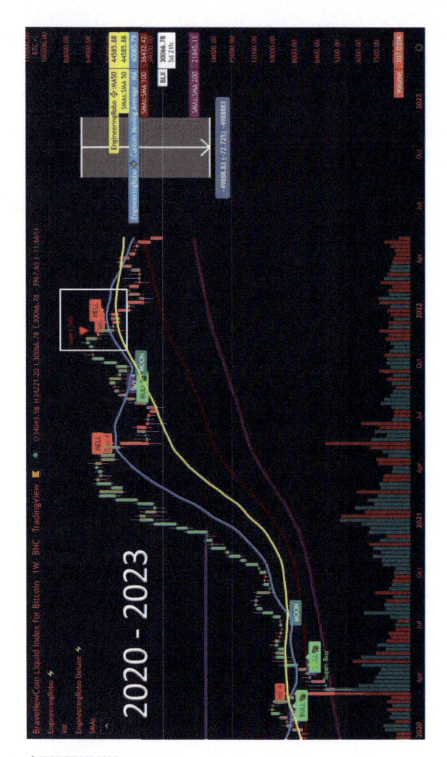

PART IX

FREQUENTLY ASKED QUESTIONS	146
10 IMPORTANT WEBSITES TO CHECK REGULARLY	151
MYTHS AND MISCONCEPTIONS FOR CRYPTO INVESTORS	153

FREQUENTLY ASKED QUESTIONS

⬤ Question: Why trade crypto with EngineeringRobo?

⬤ Answer: We always ask, "will this help our members get an edge in the market?"

When we build algorithms and set priorities, this is the first question we ask ourselves. If we have a project on the table and decide it won't give our members tangible benefits, we cut it.

1. We always invest in building world-class software!

Software is what we are all about at our core. Our software is what helps you succeed in financial markets. We'll stay focused on building the best robo advisors in the world for traders like you.

2. We empower our customers through technology and education!

Our plan for 2023 is to invest heavily in the education you need to make a living as a trader. From our articles to courses to video tutorials, we're all in on education as marketing. That's why we have created over 350 case studies on our YouTube page.

3. We enable our customers to spend less time searching for trades and more time capitalizing on them!

We are firm believers in less is more. We don't do feature wars and bloat our platform up to the hilt. Instead, we focus on the best features and do them right.

4. When you email our support team, all you have to say is "I need help" and we'll be tripping over each other to be the first ones to solve the problem for you. When you want a new feature, let us know and

we'll take the request seriously for an upcoming release. When you are part of our family, we treat you like family.

● Question: Does EngineeringRobo really work?

● Answer: Absolutely, this algorithm does really work.

However, this doesn't mean you will always generate profits, no matter what. We would never claim that EngineeringRobo guarantees to make you rich. In the world of stocks, or cryptocurrencies many things could happen. An exchange could get hacked, a security leak in a coin can be discovered, crypto can drop to $0 and governments can have a huge impact on the prices. In such situations it is not always possible to be profitable, no robo advisor, auto trading robots or manual trading strategy can be profitable if the whole market collapses.

Our Backtesting has proven that EngineeringRobo works best on markets that either bounce up and down around a certain value or markets that generally incline in value (like many coins did in 2017 and 2022). In such cases, you can beat the buy-and-hold strategy with pretty impressive results.

On markets that are steady around a certain price point, you will still see the market bounce up and down all the time because of the volatility of stocks or cryptocurrencies. Although such markets might not incline or decline much in value over time, you could still make nice profits by scalping these markets. That's what EngineeringRobo does, and there are tons of real-life examples where this has proven to be very profitable.

● Question: How does EngineeringRobo compare to competitors?

● Answer: First, we truly believe that there is no competitor offering trading tools like EngineeringRobo when it comes to simplicity and profitability. Most tools require technical knowledge or lots of documentation. We have made it our mission to bring advanced trading algorithms back to just a bunch of well-explained settings that literally anyone can use. With our highly configurable robo advisors and our unique triggers mechanism, you can create many trading strategies, from very simple buy low, sell higher strategies to more advanced strategies that automatically adapt to market movements. When it comes to functionality, there are a few competitors that also offer good trading tools. However, they are often way more expensive than EngineeringRobo. We, therefore, believe that EngineeringRobo is by far the best trading tool for what you will get.

● Question: What is the success rate of EngineeringRobo advisors?

● Answer: The success rate of EngineeringRobo advisors is from 72% to 88% on most of the 1D chart patterns.

Technical Patterns + EngineeringRobo + Resistance & Support levels = Between 80% and 85%

Technical Patterns + Resistance & Support levels + EngineeringRobo + EngineeringRobo Chat Group = Between 85% and 90%

● Question: What does 72% success mean?

● Answer: It means that 72 signals bring us to profit out of 100 signals! We will be losing money on 28 signals!

No one will ever make money 100% of the time. It's just not possible. You will endure some losing trades. But dealing with the losers and minimizing the loss incurred is what separates a good trader from a great trader. You must be mentally prepared to at some point take a loss. It's part of trading. But EngineeringRobo will show you trade management strategies to help minimize your losers and maximize your winners.

● Question: Does EngineeringRobo repaint?

● Answer: EngineeringRobo does NOT repaint, but it will flash on / off during the current bar until it closes because it is live data! The signals "can appear at any time during an open candle", but once closed the signal is final and "WON'T CHANGE" in the future. Don't enter a trade until the current bar closes with a signal if you want to be 100% sure on the signal. You enter at the opening of the succeeding candle.

● Question: Is EngineeringRobo compatible only with crypto?

● Answer: No, our products are not only compatible with Crypto, but with Stocks, Commodities and Forex as well. Get benefits by using our products for all of the above markets.

⬤ Question: Do you recommend EngineeringRobo use below the 45-minute chart?

⬤ Answer: We have back-tested robo advisors on 45M, 3H, 1D, and 1W candle charts. Below a 45-minute chart is not significant for 3 reasons: Higher time frames like 1D have less noise and are more reliable than shorter time frames like below 45M. Patterns on short-term charts can be very deceiving. Trading off a single 15-minute chart is like flying blind.

1. The extremely short time frames are very "noisy," meaning that the fluctuations in those time frames aren't very meaningful for the longer-term movement of the market.

2. Most people that trade them are scalpers, jumping in and out of the market, so they aren't the kind of people that are taking longer-term positions that would get "caught."

3. Most people, especially big-volume traders, do not trade off such short-term time frames. So, there isn't a lot of "volume" getting in and out at those swings.

For these reasons, you want to use longer-term time frames to evaluate where stops may be placed (The 15-minute chart would be the shortest for scalpers and day traders, and 3H charts would be the shortest for swing traders).

10 IMPORTANT WEBSITES TO CHECK REGULARLY

1. https://www.EngineeringRobo.com

2. https://medium.com/@engineeringrobo

3. https://www.worldcoinindex.com/trending/overview

4. https://www.cointelegraph.com

5. https://www.wewave.app/app/studio

6. https://cryptobubbles.net

7. https://www.blockchaincenter.net/en/bitcoin-rainbow-chart

8. https://rsihunter.com/ - Pick Base: USDT

9. https://www.turtlebc.com/tools/bull_percentage/btc – If the Bull Market Dominance (BTC Market) above 68% then **convert Altcoins to Bitcoin.**

10. https://www.turtlebc.com/tools/bull_percentage/usd – If the Bull Market Dominance (USDT Market) above 75% then **convert Altcoins to USDT.**

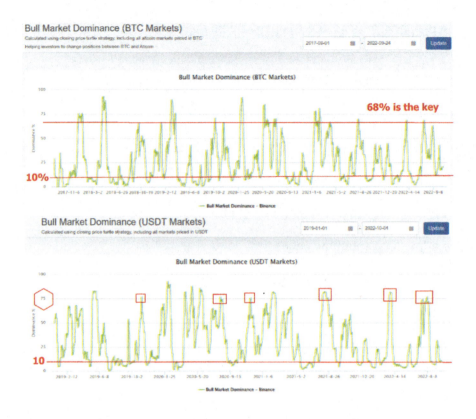

🎯 **Pro-tip:** If the Bull Market dominance (BTC Markets) is below 10% convert your Bitcoin to Altcoins.
If the Bull Market dominance (BTC Markets) is above 68% convert your Altcoins to Bitcoin.

🎯 **Pro-tip:** If the Bull Market dominance (USDT Markets) is below 10% convert USDT to Altcoins.
If the Bull Market dominance (USDT Markets) is above below 75% convert Altcoins to USDT.

MYTHS AND MISCONCEPTIONS FOR CRYPTO INVESTORS

There are some myths and misconceptions about investing in cryptocurrencies. In order for you to have a better understanding of what it really means to be a crypto investor, be sure that you know the truth behind the myths: Investing in cryptocurrencies is gambling!

This is one of the reasons why people shy away from the crypto market. However, this is not always true. Take note that the prices of crypto in the market depend on certain factors, such as the economy, business partnerships, supply and demand, and technological developments, among others. The prices of cryptocurrencies do not fluctuate randomly. There are always reasons behind every movement. This is unlike gambling in a casino where the outcome of a game depends on a shuffled deck of cards that nobody has any idea how each card is positioned on the deck.

Whether the crypto market is gambling or not depends on how you approach it. Of course, if you simply pick the cryptos at random and merely rely on pure luck to be successful, then you are gambling. As such, you can expect the same results as you would when you gamble in the casino. However, if you approach the crypto market professionally where you put in enough time, and effort, and follow EngineeringRobo signals, in your every transaction, if you consider every act as an investment decision, then you are not gambling but investing. Gamblers rely on luck, while true investors know what they are doing and have an edge over the crypto market.

1. Investing in cryptocurrencies will make you a multi-millionaire overnight

Investing in cryptos is just like any other business: You can make money; however, you can also lose money. Like any investment, there are risks involved. Indeed, there are people who are able to grow their money, but there are also many investors who lose their money. To be successful, you need to understand the crypto market and apply certain strategies. Of course, a major part of success is to conduct serious knowledge.

It is also worth noting that you will only earn a certain percentage of your investment. Of course, it is possible that you earn more than 1000% or even 10,000% of your investment. However, do not expect it to happen overnight. Therefore, the more money you invest, the more profit you can make.

2. The crypto market is only for speculators or rich people

Some think that you can only invest in cryptocurrencies if you belong to a particular exclusive group. This is not true. The crypto market is open to everyone provided you are of legal age, and there are no other legal prohibitions applicable to you in your state. Especially today where you can invest in cryptos by simply opening an account with an online crypto exchange, you can invest even with as little as $100, or even less.

3. An easy way to make money

Since you just have to pick cryptos and invest in some money, wait for some time, and then sell to enjoy your profits, then making money with the crypto market must be easy, right? I am afraid that is not the case. Although you can do all these with just a few clicks of a mouse, investing in cryptocurrencies is not as simple as it looks. The main problem lies in choosing the right cryptocurrencies to invest in, as well as following the proper robo-advisors.

4. Start investing in demo accounts

Demo trading is useless "unless" you're Backtesting Engineeringrobo signals. In the demo, you can trade without experimental psychological pressure. We have also heard from people that, after using the demo account, it is not easy to transition to the real one. Completely different conditions. With that being said, we do not recommend our members trade on demo accounts.

AFTERWORD

On a personal note, I believe this book has shed light on the complexities of the trading industry. Trading is my passion, and I'm glad I've had the opportunity to share it with you. While I hardly expect all readers of this book to transform themselves into super-traders—the world just doesn't work that way—I believe you have learned from this book that trading successfully, like most things in life, takes a lot of hard work and dedication.

Even after you have learned all of the skills set forth in this book, at some point in time it will probably occur to you that your trading is simply a feedback mechanism to tell you how much you like yourself at any given moment. The more positive you feel about yourself, the more abundance will naturally flow your way as a by-product of these positive feelings. So, in essence, to give yourself more money as a trader you need to identify, change or discharge anything in your mental environment that doesn't contribute to the highest degree of self-valuation that is possible.

What's possible? Stay focused on what you need to learn, and do the work that is necessary, and your belief in what is possible will naturally expand as a function of your willingness to adapt.

Noted business guru Jim Rohn has been quoted as saying, "We must all suffer from one of two pains: the pain of discipline or the pain of regret. The difference is discipline weighs ounces, while regret weighs tons." I believe this statement directly applies to active trading: you will not succeed as an active trader without a significant amount of discipline. The EngineeringRobo system that I've laid out in this book is simple, but it's not easy. If you follow the rules that I explained here, I genuinely believe that you will succeed. These rules aren't easy. In the heat of the moment, it's tempting to deviate from these rules and make up your own. Don't give in to such temptation—I assure you that it will be your downfall. These rules are specifically set up to maximize your gains and minimize your losses.

Keeping your cool, and your discipline, and continuing to learn about active trading will place you on the right path to becoming a great trader. Ultimately, active trading is a demanding profession that requires proper training. Visit www.EngineeringRobo.com for even more information on furthering your trading career.

Thank you, and happy trading!

EngineeringRobo

INDEX

1% Rule, 44, 46
Algo Trading, 74, 75
Backtesting, 81, 83, 85, 147, 155
Blockchain, 9, 12, 13, 15, 25
Commodities, 29, 69, 79, 122, 149
Dollar-Cost Averaging, 41, 42
Economy, 4, 153
Fibonacci, 70, 79
Finance, 1, 2, 34, 76, 77, 116
Golden Cross, 72, 80, 86, 94
Hedge Funds, 21
High-Frequency Trading (HFT), 3, 31
Mentor, 50, 87, 97, 100, 131
NFT, 20, 123

Other People's Money (OPM), 58
Portfolio Management Tool, 52, 53, 94
Risk-Reward, 45
Robot, 3, 74, 75, 76, 78, 147
Satoshi Nakamoto, 11, 12
Scalping, 31, 37, 38, 53, 147
South Sea Bubble, 127, 128
Stop-Loss, 44, 45, 46, 53, 74, 80
Three-Strike Rule, 37
Wall Street, 64, 78, 116, 117, 118, 119
Wealth, 18, 30, 116, 117, 119, 127, 131

REFERENCES

[1] http://www.academy.binance.com

[2] http://www.investopedia.com

[3] http://www.tradingview.com

[4] http://www.cointelegraph.com

[5] http://www.money.yahoo.com

TO GET FUTURE UPDATES, FOLLOW US ON...

YouTube: https://www.youtube.com/c/EngineeringRobo

Telegram Group: https://t.me/EngineeringRobo

Twitter: https://twitter.com/EngineeringRobo

Instagram: https://www.instagram.com/Engineeringrobo

Facebook: https://www.facebook.com/EngineeringRobo

Tradingview: https://www.tradingview.com/u/EngineeringRobo

Medium: https://medium.com/@Engineeringrobo

Steemit: https://steemit.com/@Engineeringrobo

Publish0x: https://www.publish0x.com/Engineeringrobo

TikTok: https://www.tiktok.com/@engineeringrobo

WhatsApp: https://wa.me/message/ROMBUJSUNXDME1

Stocktwits: https://stocktwits.com/EngineeringRobo

Odysse LBRY: https://odysee.com/@EngineeringRobo

Website: https://www.engineeringrobo.com

Printed by Amazon Italia Logistica S.r.l.
Torrazza Piemonte (TO), Italy